Ph!losoph!cal Incl!nat!ons

*Bringing the Poise of Your Divine Nature to the
Noise of Materiality*

Bil Holton

Prosperity Publishing House
Durham, NC

Prosperity Publishing House
    Durham, NC
Library of Congress Cataloging-in-Publication Data
Holton, Bil
My Mystical Moments Musings / Bil Holton
p. cm.

ISBN 978-1-946291-24-0 (Print-softcover)
ISBN 978-1-946291-25-7 (eBook)
ISBN 978-1-946291-26-4 (Kindle)

1. Spiritual   2. New Thought   3. Self Help

II. Title

Library of Congress Control Number: 2025942268
Printed in the United States of America

To my incredible wife, Cher,
who sees the 'greater good' value
in my higher consciousness flights of fancy –
and to my devoted New Thought readers
over the years who see the value in bringing the poise
of their Divine Nature to the noise of materiality.

Table of Contents

Preface

As I thought about what higher consciousness ph!losoph!cal !ncl!nat!ons to include in this book for those who, like me, want to bring the poise of their Divine Nature to the noise of materiality, I wanted to increase the bandwidth of the printed and/or digital landscape as well, so that it complemented my sometimes playful, other times serious thought process.

So, you'll see that throughout this book I've occasionally played with spelling, the spacing between letters, and even made up some new words—all to illustrate there's something novel at play. And, as you've probably already noticed, the book title itself is no exception.

As a matter of explanation, my book title, *Ph!losoph!cal !ncl!nat!ons,* uses 'inverted or proxied space' instead of 'negative space' to emphasize the expansive philosophical nature of the book's content. As you can readily see, the exclamation point substitutes for the 'i's' in the title. I've also occasionally used 'inverted or proxied space' through-out the book to reinforce the out-of-the-box theme.

Here's how I arrived at the 'inverted and proxied space nuance: In art and design, for instance, *negative space* is the background space around and between the subject of an image. Check out art and design logos like FedEx, Spade Dealer, Bateman, Pittsburg Zoo & PPG Aquarium, etc. You can also use what we call 'proxied space,' which substitutes such icons as the '$' and @ for an 's' and an 'a' respectively. (As an aside, you can also use proxied space in creating unique passwords.)

Who Should Read This Book

Okay. Enough of a preamble! This book is written for those who don't, won't, wouldn't ever hesitate to question unquestioned answers, who honor evidenced-based truths instead of buying into proselytized beliefs that intentionally retail fiction and misinformation. This book is about spirituality, psience,[1] and science, not about the siloed, inquisitional outbursts of scientism proponents, which seems to have both a psi[2] phobia and religion loathing.

For those who specialize in toilsome confirmation biases and truant dogmas (unenlightened allergies), I suggest that you may want to think twice about reading this book. It'll challenge anyone with embedded confirmation biases and who specializes in the hubris of unbridled dogmatic bloating that's based on misinformation and disinformation. It'll expose the fiction leakage in their preconceived, nonsensical, evidence-barren beliefs and lame biases. However, if you have the courage to question unquestioned answers and enough open-mindedness to challenge your own assumptions and biases, the transformative content in this book will elevate your rational thinking, being and doing to a higher consciousness octave.

This isn't the book, nor am I the author, for people who choose to perpetually ignore questioning unquestioned answers. I'm not the kind of guy who validates dogmatic nonsense, which I kick to the curb every chance I get! A quip attributed to one of my favorite authors, Mark Twain, speaks to the idiocy of truant dogmas: "It ain't what you don't know that gets you into trouble. It's what you know for sure that just ain't so."

My purpose for writing this book is ph!losoph!cally !ncl!ned in order to stimulate open-minded, forward thinking people to embrace higher thought processes that lead to nirvanic enlightenment. As a matter of fact, the word 'philosopher' (first used by Pythagoras) means 'lover of Sophia (wisdom)'!

I feel a ph!losoph!cal book like this will not be complete until it becomes panoptically a nucleus of its readers' expanding consciousness and enlightened perspective on the nature of Reality Itself. As this book's subtitle suggests, I invite you to bring the poise of your Divine Nature to the noise of materiality in every waking moment.

Once again, for those who already question unquestioned answers and challenge the status quo, I hope you'll enjoy the read and be stimulated by many of my ph!losoph!cal perspectives.

[1] Psience (my term) is the systematic study of psi phenomena through observation and experiment, seeing it as one of the 'pair' of normals: normal physical realities and supernormal ethereal realities. Psi is from the Greek word for Spirit or Soul.

[2] British psychologist Robert Thouless adopted the term 'psi' in 1942.

Ph!losoph!cal Exploration

Whether you're reading these posts digitally or atomically, I welcome you and hope my ph!losoph!cal !ncl!nat!ons spur your own. And as you turn (or swipe) these pages, I invite you to fully enjoy exploring your own neuroverse and psiverse so you can create your future— rather than simply react to it. Let each post (entry) create an opportunity for reflection, questioning, and deep-dive thought. Are you ready? Let's dive in together!

* * * * * * *

Brain Weaver

Be a 'brain weaver,' a 'psioneer*' experient. Make each of these brain weaving practices a habit for optimum brain health and over-all bodily well-being: aerobic and anaerobic exercise; a plant-based, non-inflammatory food and drink diet; probiotics; proper amount of sleep and rest; questioning unquestioned answers; meditation and affirmative prayer; evidence-based integrative medicines and supplements; re-parenting your Inner Child; making left and right brain hemispheric synchronization a daily practice; positive thinking; affirmations; homeopathic remedies; brain fitness games; dumping all forms of derelict, indigestible dogma; healthy breathing techniques; yawning to cool the brain; stress reduction; making mystical moments and extrasensory psi experiences a legitimate part of your over-all spiritual psioneering practice.

> * I created the word 'psioneer' to describe someone who enjoys exploring mystical and unexplainable phenomena, psychic abilities, and events that are experienced without hard evidence to back them up.

Going Public With Private Knowing

Ph!losoph!cally speaking, this book and the one I wrote just before it (*My Mystical Moment Musings*) are my way of going public with private knowing. And while much of my 'knowing' related to my mystical and psi experiences has been more self-evidentiary than laboratory digitizable, I know, as an experient of psi sleuthing, that the psiverse (Phantastic Supersensory Intelligence) is absolutely real. These two books, as of this writing, are the public demonstrations of my personal psioneering experiences and psi-related research that have contributed to my over-all soul growth and spiritual depth.

It Can Be Brutiful At Times

Mind auction can be *brutiful* at times, but when it moves toward mind action you'll find that the process is worth it.

Astronomically Speaking

Two things are astronomical: our universe and humankind's penchant for not questioning unquestioned answers!

Memeplexes

The multiplicity of viral god memes (memeplexes) throughout human history have perpetuated (replicated and shared) the unfortunate idea of primitive anthropomorphic deities that sell fear, guilt and shame, thus keeping humankind habitually vulnerable to nasty dogma bites.

Science Friction

When it comes to questioning unquestioned answers, challenging religious beliefs and science fiction usually leads to religious and science friction.

Desiring the Best

Desiring the best generally trumps desiring merely the good.

Raising Our Are-ness

It's no doubt clear to you by now that raising our Consciousness requires raising our Are-ness to reach our Isness! Just like our brain merely records and registers what our mind sends to it, we must simply raise our awareness, receptivity and energy at the human level (our Are-ness) in order to express our Pure Universal Consciousness Nature (our Isness).

Out-Datedness vs. Up-Datedness

Spirituality, psience, and science generally run counter to religion's hyper-dogmatic mindset (based on unenlightened allergies), because most religions* rely solely on unchanging, outdated teachings and writings, while spirituality, psience, and science constantly update their findings in order to avoid swimming in bogus dogmatic language and joining others under dogmatic umbrellas. There, I've said it. I'm purposefully pre-bunking truant dogmas freighted with evidence-barren suppositions and beliefs.

> * As of this writing, there appears to be around 4,200 different religions on the planet.

Let It Sync In

Allow the cosmic twinship of your Human Nature and your Divine Nature to sync in!

Cluttered Emptiness

If a *cluttered* desk or computer desktop is a sign of a cluttered mind, what, then, is an *empty* desk or desktop a sign of?

Gaba Dabba Doo

We humans are literally marvels of infiniteness mixed with finiteness, suspended on the webbing of our neuroverse and bioverse in human form. For example, our brain's calming chemical is called gamma-aminobutyric acid (GABA)—a sort of morphine, marijuana and valium cocktail.

It relieves anxiety, improves mood, and treats attention deficit-hyperactivity disorder (ADHD), and is also used for promoting lean muscle growth, burning fat, stabilizing blood pressure, and relieving pain. Interesting how our body adapts to its environment and creates coping mechanisms to protect us and sustain us.

You probably recognize our 'gaba dabba doo' spin-off from the iconic catchphrase 'Yabba-Dabba-Doo' which was the cartoon character, Fred Flintstone's way of expressing excitement and exuberance.

Soul Growth Rescue Work

Remembering old hurts and upsets and then replacing them with positive mental and emotional rewrites is soul growth rescue work.

Self-ishness

Some people think (unjustifiably) they're being selfish because they feel good when they help others. However, when you capitalize the letter 'S' in 'self' and add a dash between the 'f' and 'i' the implication is you're being Self-ish (aligning your Human Self with your Divine Self via an *Arhatic** Yoga perspective). Being Self-ish is being just the opposite of selfish. That cosmic alignment is silk for the soul!

> * *Arhatic* derives from the Sanskrit word '*Arhat,*' which means a 'perfected one' or 'highly evolved being.' Arhatis Yoga marries teachings from Buddhism, Theosophy, yoga, qigon, and esoteric Christianity.

PTSD

Familiar initials? Right? Well it depends on the context! It generally stands for 'post-traumatic stress disorder.' However, The 'P' in this familiar series of letters could refer to the sixteenth letter of the Greek alphabet, which stands for Pi* (Π, π). And given that analogy, PTSD could read as: Pi To Six Digits, which would be 314159! Isn't that cool! Acronyms are a matter of perspective based on their context.

Pi is a mathematical constant and could also refer to the ratio of a circle's circumference to its diameter, and it also has various equivalent definitions. It's been represented by the Greek letter 'π' since the mid-18th century, and is spelled out as 'pi.' It's also referred to as Archimedes' constant.

The Quantum and Classical Worlds

One question quantum physicists and parapsychologists are asking is: Is there quantum and psi-ness in the classical world? Classical Newtonian mechanics deals with things that are larger - generally large enough to see, and quantum physics deals with things that are tiny - a nanometer or less, which is the size of atoms. The nature of entanglement seems to be the key to the weirdness of both.

By analogy, from a spiritual point of view: To what degree are our human physicality and psi-ness commingled (entangled) with Omnipresent Divinity? And also, the thought has occurred to me, what type of entanglement will there be in the new physics which will lie beyond both of the current physics ideologies?

If Money Were No Object

Many people ask: "If money were no object, what would I do?" The thing is—money IS an object! It's the chief currency in skin school. There's a need to make money—a certain amount of money to live comfortably and pro$perou$ly! So, a better question to ask yourself might be: "Knowing I need to attract a certain amount of income to maintain the lifestyle I want, what can I do to accomplish that?"

Super-Sensual Intoxications

While I recognize that I'm a more spiritual minister than scientist, I've found that you must transcend your parochial physical sense world in order to experience the 'super-sensual intoxications' of powerful mystical insperiences, because it's there that you'll enter the innermost sanctuary of your exquisite transpersonal beingness. Each mystical, insperiential moment of deep silence (*silentium altum*) is a testimony of an incredible psi experience, because it tunes down the noise of external stimuli.

Tree of Life

Our Divine Nature is the Eternal Tree of Life leafing Itself as us in human form.

Retreat Forward

Purposefully sequester yourself into a few moments of quiet solitude and use meditation as an intuitive 'retreat forward' as you start each day. It's starting your day on the left foot (the right brain hemisphere). MetaSpiritually, your left foot symbolizes deep spiritual understanding and your right foot stands for accumulating spiritual knowledge.

The Still Point

This post is worth sitting up straight and taking a couple of slow breaths to read! The Still Point, the Spiritual Singularity within you, is where your intuitive wisdom and Super-Consciousness (Supersentience) live. Visit it every chance you get. It'll keep you above the fray of indecisiveness, worry and wrong turns as you matriculate through your skin school experiences.

The Negative Return Mode

In space shuttle launches, the 'negative return' refers to a specified point during second-stage ascent, that Mission Control will make a non-abort call to the crew indicating their status with respect to aborts. For example, the 'negative return' call indicates that it's too late to select a return-to-launch-site (RTLS) abort.

When it comes to our soul growth, the 'negative return mode' refers to when we get to a certain level of higher spiritual understanding and appreciation of higher cosmic Truths, there's no going back to a delinquent dogmatic religious perspective which touts, among other things, a primitively anthropomorphic god meme in the sky.

Escape Velocity

According to NASA, a space craft's escape velocity at launch must be 25,000 mph to free itself from Earth's gravitational pull. MetaSpiritually speaking, the escape velocity (courage, commonsense, wisdom, levelheaded discernment) for soaring past the gravitational pull of rooted religious and scientific dogmas is the speed of more enlightened thought.

Cell-ebrate Cell Power

We have the pharmacy of pharmacies built into our DNA—and we have the intelligence of the universe distributed throughout our body within the diversity of the cells that constitute our bio-makeup. Cher and I invite you to partner with your cellular family. Maintain a loving, mutually-satisfying, symbiotic relationship. Cell-ebrate your cell power. Within your cellular genealogy is your *wholing* genie-ology! Experience the awesome wholeness, wholesomeness and holiness that come from the reciprocity between 'self to cell' and 'cell to self.'

Truthizing Yourself

You're both ancestor and heir, host and guest, guru and student to your continued spiritual growth. You're not only a multi-storied spiritual being, you're a multi-dimensional quantum being. Knowing this about yourself is truthizing yourself.

Breaking the Light Barrier

Humankind has already broken the sound barrier. As we become more supersentient, will we be able to break the light barrier (travel faster than the speed of light)? I believe we have the capacity to do that when it comes to figuring out space travel! However, the 'Light' I'm referring to is the 'Inner Light' of our Divine Nature which is the individualized 'Light Beam' (Life Force) of the of the Omnipresent Universal Reality actualizing as us in our lower vibrational carbon-based form, so we can travel faster than the speed of human error.

The Prayerful Petitioning of Memeology

Petitioning prayers which focus on begging (beseeching, pleading, asking, etc.) a primitive anthropomorphic Judeo-Christian God meme for His (this meme is usually referred to as a He) assistance and favor, are for the consumption of the dogmatic religious faithful only.

Subluminality

To me, our universe and its neighboring universes and multiverses, must be subluminal* properties of a Universal Omnipresent Consciousness.

* Subluminal means slower than the speed of light.

The Zen Inclusive Mind State

You learn that there're many levels of alpha and gamma overtones. At a 'oneness with all' level there seems to be a spacetime detachment. Even the sensation of separation from the material universe occurs, a feeling of becoming aware of the unifying thread of all life. There's a Zen-ness, an instant satori, that the filling of the head with alpha and gamma waves with their accompanying divorcement from material reality is the equivalent of what I call the Zen inclusive mind state. This inclusive mindfulness is the absence of thoughts of material attachments, a dissolution of any material restrictions, a faster than the speed of lightness. You experience an ecstatic, mystical state of unity with the multidimensional universe.

The Mystical Moment Envelope

I got the idea for the 'mystical moment envelope' from an insight I received in a dream I had a week after the horrible incident at the Capital Building on Jan. 6, 2021. The insight during my dream was 'sleep in an envelope' which was a saying introduced around twenty years ago. I had never heard it before, but the dream fragment inspired me to investigate the old adage.

It turns out that the idea means there's not one single element of your bed that's the key to a good night's sleep, but rather every piece works in unison to create the ideal environment to catch some shut eye. (For example, a metal base, mattress, waterproof encasement, fitted sheet, comforter, blanket, three pillows, regular pillow case, hypoallergenic pillow encasement, washable wool pillow cover, etc.)

A similar thing applies to experiencing fantastic mystical moments—or meditation, déjà vu, visualization, trance, epiphany experiences. There's more than one single element associated with those experiences that produces stunning revelations. (For example, desire to connect with your true spiritual essence; proper breathing; open-mindedness; a more spiritual, not religious orientation; privacy; access to your super-consciousness; being calm and relaxed; a gammatized [40-60 Hz amplitude] and/or alphatized [8-14 Hz amplitude] state of mind, openness to new possibilities, light hypnotic propensity; comfortable seating and/or tranquil movement; etc.)

In-Sync-ness

People are looking everywhere for stimulus packages and bail out programs, but Cher and I'll put our money on our Divine Nature's in sync ness with the Field of Infinite Potential.

Pretzel Poses

Yoga and sitting meditations aren't about getting into impossible pretzel poses. They're not about getting yourself tied up into knots. On the contrary, their efficacy is a non-pretzeled and uncomplicated inner life.

Unapologetically Inclined

As a MetaSpiritually-oriented and esoterically inclined ph!losopher, I'm interested in everything interesting! And I make no apologies for those spontaneous inclinations.

15

Innertainment

Ph!losoph!z!ng, mystical experiences, reveries, revelations, Aha moments, trance states, meditations, visualizations, musings, lucid dreams and daydreams, past life regressions, apparitions, phantasmas, etc., are all forms of innertainment.

Anomaly Sleuthing

When you think about it, interest in physics anomalies (things faster than the speed of light, dark matter and dark energy, ghost particles, not-so-constant constants, megacryometeors falling from sky, etc.), medical anomalies (placebo effect, sudoku seizures, toothy brain, star in the eye cataract, excessive generosity, gluten delusions, spontaneous human combustion, etc.). and geography anomalies (mysterious hot spots on the Great Pyramid, ancient underwater highway off the coast of the Bahamas, Chocolate Hills of the Philippines, Rainbow Mts. In Zhangye Danxia, spoked wheel structures in the Azraq Oasis, crop circles, etc.).

I'm also including Higher Consciousness anomalies, what I call Phantastic Supersensory Intelligence or psi (mystical experiences, déjà vu experiences, lucid dreams, human-to-human telepathy, human-to-pet telepathy, remote viewing, hallucinations, OBEs and NDEs, trance states, precognitive dreams, precognition, deep meditation, synchronicity, epiphanies, stigmata, receiving memories and personality traits from organ donors, children who remember past lives incidents (CWRPLs), lives between lives episodes, astral projection, spontaneous recoveries, life reviews, bodily levitation, etc.), could be considered anomaly sleuthing.

Ph!losoph!cal Excitation

Ph!losoph!cal !ncl!nat!ons are self-excitatory moments that lead to panoptic ph!losoph!cal perspectives, which lead to ph!losoph!cal meanderings, that lead to ph!losoph!cal revelations, that lead to more ph!losoph!zing, which leads to … you get the point!

Psi Shock

Psi shock is the dizzying disorientation brought on by the unexpected sudden arrival of a psi event in one's life that seems to have come out of nowhere. The surfacing of psi abilities (psi architecture), like telepathy, clairvoyance, precognition, etc., you didn't know you possessed could very well become new normal for you. Perhaps one day we humans will regularize psi abilities as more people try the 'psi pside' of life!

A Good Heir Day

Neuroscientists tell us that most of our decisions, actions, emotions and behavior depend on what's recorded in our subconsciousness. This means that 95% of our thinking and behavior is influenced by the composite programming in our prepackaged subconscious mind.

That means, depending on what subconscious 'voices' we listen to, we can have a good heir day or a bad heir day. Now hear me right—I said good heir day (HEIR day) or bad heir day (HEIR day). We're the HEIR of our past thoughts, biases, beliefs, choices, and behaviors.

Perpetual Fiction

The price we pay for disinterest and indifference to questioning unquestioned answers is living in perpetual fiction.

The Right Stuff

The right stuff today can make up for a bout of the goofy stuff of yesterday.

Mystical Moment Insperiences

I feel somewhat at a loss to describe my mystical insperiences, because they've all been incredibly *ex--pan---sive* experiences which defy reductionist explanations. And the experiences themselves are soooo incredibly phenomenal that their ineffability quotient makes it difficult to express what I've just experienced in coherent words.

Expressing my comprehension in words describing the other-worldly reality I just experienced would require me to invent a new language that would describe a totally new experience that the people who didn't have the experience could understand. Even after thinking about the experience, it would still be difficult coming up with a description that would do it justice. Extremely personalized sensory 'nakedness' is extremely difficult to cloth in language. However, I believe putting suitable labels on phenomenal mystical experiences is possible. It'll mean inventing extrasensory-specific language to do an end run around its built-in ineffability.

The YOUniversal Us

Getting in touch with other geographies as we travel, reminds us of our own inner landscape. As John Primack and Nancy Ellen Abrams remind us in their splendid book, *The View From the Center of the Universe*:

Each of us is an atomic pastiche: the iron atoms in our blood carrying oxygen at this moment to our cells came largely from exploding white dwarf stars, while the oxygen itself came mainly from exploding supernovas that ended the lives of massive stars, and most of the carbon in the carbon dioxide we exhale on every breath came from planetary nebulas, the death clouds of middle-sized stars a little bigger than our sun. We are made of material created and ejected into the Galaxy by the violence of earlier stars. Human beings are made of the rarest material in the universe: stardust. Except for hydrogen, which makes up about a tenth of our weight, the rest of our body is stardust. Our bodies literally have the entire history of the universe, witnessed and enacted by our atoms.

Cher and I thought you'd appreciate your own atomic *pasticheness* and interstellar oneness as a universal cosmic being. We're one with the universe and the universe is one with us. As a YOUniverse, we're an imitation of the universe, using its subatomic and atomic parts to form our own version of the Omnipresent Universal Reality.

Our Physical Envelopes

Our consciousness isn't lost after each incarnational/ reincarnational experience in spite of the dissolution of our physical envelopes, because our physicality is a product of our crystalizing consciousness. One of the tasks of our incarnational selves is to learn to master our physical envelopes. And one of the products of expanding the bandwidth of our awareness in each of our physical envelopes is to recognize that truth.

The Dream Realm

What if dreams are desires chased in sleep?

My Ph!losoph!cal-Esque Tendencies

I had grown up in a household where the original Twilight Zone series was my preferred TV watching, my church going was forced religious dogmatism, but my chosen 'babysitter' was the Theosophical Society literature. Is it any wonder that I've happily gravitated toward becoming a New Thought minister, am interested in quantum physics, and have a ph!losoph!cal-esque penchant for questioning any-and- all unquestioned answers?

Here-apy or There-apy

One of the best 'therapies' I can offer our hyperdogmatic religious friends is that G.O.D. (an acronym for Global Omnipresent Divinity) is 'here-apy' (actualizing within us and as us in human form) and not 'there-apy' (an anthropomorphic being separate from us).

Ice-Cream Cone Wisdom

Work without joy is as hollow as an empty ice-cream cone.

The Secrets of Psi

The secrets of psi are awaiting our continued, open-minded research, enthusiastic personal receptivity and experience, and altruistic use.

See No Evil, Hear No Evil, Speak No Evil

Seeing no evil, hearing no evil, and speaking no evil would be a terrific human species-specific achievement, don't you think! You notice we didn't end that statement with a question mark.

It's one of our greatest hopes that humankind will embrace the opposite of 'evil' and collectively 'LIVE' at a higher vibrational order of beingness that's characterized by unconditional love, compassion, kindness, mutual respect, and so on—so we can support one another throughout our collective skin school experience. Unfortunately, as of this writing, it looks like when it comes to eliminating 'evil-doings' in general, the human race has had more won't power than will power!

Vizsponsibly

Most people aren't aware of how powerful visualizing can be in their lives. In fact, many people are doing plenty of visualizations every day whether they realize it or not. Visualization isn't something woo woo used by people who have lost touch with reality. It's quite the opposite; it's used by a people who recognize its higher consciousness value.

Essentially, our subconscious mind is a programmable 'hard drive.' Our subconscious 'programs' are largely stimulus-response behaviors which are downloaded (warehoused) into our subconscious via our conscious thoughts, choices and behaviors. And the neat thing about it is our subconsciousness doesn't rely on the outside world for its 'knowing,' because it doesn't differentiate between what's real and what's imagined.

Our visualizations reprogram old beliefs and eliminate negative patterns. Although we may still remember a negative event, our emotional response changes. The attachment we once had is essentially eliminated. When we change our belief we change our response to life and what we believe we can achieve. That's what visualizations do for us! So, in a very real sense, we have an obligation, a responsibility to visualize responsibly (Cher and I call it *vizsponsiblity*) to create a better life for ourselves.

Wheelies

Here are a couple of my mus!ngs about the invention of the wheel:

What if, instead of inventing the wheel to get us from point 'A' to point 'B' humankind learned how to bilocate?

It's occurred to me that whoever invented the first wheel was a nincompoop. The person who invented the other three, was a genius!

Recloaking Ourselves

When you think about it, our reincarnations are a rebooting. They're recloaking ourselves in a different physical embodiment for our next skin school experience.

The Über-DNA of the Tao

I'm convinced that all living things constitute the Über-DNA of the Tao. I prefix the DNA reference with the German word Über, because as I've indicated earlier Über means 'higher or Super-Conscious.' And that's what this insight that came to me after a mystical moment in the Spring of 2019 is all about. The evolution of sentient consciousness is the birthing of DNA's complexity, frequency elevation, and Species-Specific entanglement. When a member of a specific species elevates its conscious awareness, the entire hive consciousness (collective consciousness) of that species is raised an octave.

It's Everywhere

Your Divine Nature is everywhere you are! Sooo …

MetaSpiritual Coinage

MetaSpiritual is a word Cher and I coined in 2015 to describe a higher consciousness neuroverse characterized by evidence-based science and psience, faith-based spirituality, and metaphor-based metaphysics. After coining the term 'MetaSpiritual,' we discovered Teilhard de Chardin's term 'hyperphysics' which means pretty much the same thing as MetaSpiritual just before Christmas in 2020. Chardin saw 'hyperphysics' as a kind of metaphysics, but beyond metaphysics, that springs from the hard sciences. Like Chardin, we have a science-based bent that complements our higher consciousness spiritual perspective.

We're Family

Every living thing, no matter how much it differs from other living things in physical appearance, 'speaks' almost exactly the 'same language' when it comes to genes. This strongly supports that all organisms are descended from a single common ancestor. Sooo, all life forms are related to one another. We're family!

Surreal

Surreal isn't a cute way of saying 'cereal.'

Talk is Cheap?

If you think talk is cheap and texting is economical, check out your smart phone bills.

Junking-Up Our Consciousness

The higher consciousness aspects and expanded bandwidth of a more enlightened, anomaly-enhanced, MetaSpiritual perspective gives us the common language we need to make better sense of our cosmic nature and the true nature of Reality. A religious mindset can't do that, because it blocks any chance of a transcendental view of the true nature of Reality by failing to see beyond its high-walled, indigestible dogmas.

We must refrain from junking-up our consciousness with dogmafication (not questioning stale conventional answers that are based on falsehoods). As spiritual beings we're collectively tasked with keeping our neuroverses free from dogmatic junk so we can gain the clarity we need to grow our spirituality.

Subconscious Archeology

Our subconsciousness in our current skin school experience is 'neuro-shared space' with our past lives' composite consciousness and the combined consciousness patterns, propensities, and biases of our current multidimensional selves. When you think about it, when we dig into our subconscious prepackaged patterns it's called subconscious archeology. The old habits and patterns are past lives' artifacts that we've held onto for many incarnations. We get to decide what we consider as treasures, what we want to keep, and what we need to toss.

A 'Glass Act'

We downsized the number of glasses we had in the house this week. We hadn't used any of them in, we're embarrassed to say, a couple of years! It turned out to be quite a 'glass act!'

Your Somatic Spacetime Suit

Be absolutely clear about this, your human body is a garment (camouflage) you wear to clothe your choice to become the physical being that you are. It's your biological address. It's the 'somatic space suit' you've constructed to house your particular version of Spirit.

For Your Dining Pleasure

Meditations and writing are good after-breakfast snacks. MetaSpiritual discussions are excellent lunch entrées, and ph!losoph!cal !ncl!nat!ons are wonderful evening meals and desserts.

Plural Realities

It seems obvious there are plural subjective realities, not only among the human species, but those realities where every living thing lives. Sooo, is there really an Omnipresent Universal Reality that every sentient living thing can get in touch with—and get in touch with at the same time? Or does the Omnipresent Universal Reality require Supersentience?

Cellular Theology

Each cell, every molecule, each of your atoms is a sacred tabernacle of Pure Consciousness. These sacred tabernacles are connected and they're highly intelligent beings. There is no Interfaith posturing. Their biology is their theology. When you realize the significance of this invisible connection you'll honor your human soul's relationship to your *Higher Spiritual Self.* When you acknowledge this connection, from soul to cell and from cell to soul, your body becomes the highly-charged sacred ground of your being. When you achieve this perfect synchrony you'll experience the inner peace, joy, health, and wholeness which are the truth of you. So, cell-ebrate your cell power!

Global Morality

If humankind can agree on a global morality, what would it look like?

Dowsing For Tao-sing

As you probably already know, dowsing is a type of divination that's used to locate ground water, oil, buried material, invisible objects, etc. You may not know its relationship to Tao-sing (a term we've coined)! Suppose 'Tao-sing,' which is divining the absolute principle (Path, the Way) underlying the universe. That is, it combines within itself the principles of yin and yang which divine the hidden harmony and higher order supersentient vibrations of the invisible realms of the natural order of the universe?

> *The scientific explanation for what happens when people dowse is the 'ideomotor phenomenon' in psychology—muscle movements caused by subconscious mental activity that make anything held in one's hands move. It looks and feels as if the movements are involuntary. The same phenomenon has been shown to lie behind movements of objects during Ouija boarding.

From Homogenized to Non-Dairy

Believe it or not, the path to Full Enlightenment means going from homogenized, hyperdogmatic religion to differentiated non-dairy spirituality.

Confidential Health Advisors

Confidential health advisors are the pacemakers, glucose monitors, an actual illness or dis-ease, unusual aches and pains, fevers, feelings of 'something not rightness' we get when we listen to our bodies, temperature thermometers, etc.

Ph!losoph!cally Speaking

I'm driven by two main ph!losoph!cal !ncl!nat!ons: to unhesitatingly 'up my consciousness' so I can better align my Human Nature with my Divine Nature, and be instrumental in lessening the suffering of others.

Flight Into Solitude

As we looked at where we are spiritually—allegorically, metaphysically, philosophically, and MetaSpiritually—and where the majority of humankind is in terms of its almost complete unawareness of its Divine Nature, Cher and I wondered how much difference we could make in helping the world awaken to its True Spiritual Nature. There have been many people (outliers), far superior to us in intellect and influential positions of authority who helped form the basis of our rarified spiritual perspective, but were themselves unable to ease humankind out of its slumber. Many of these outliers went into seclusion - or were forced into it, by a world society that refused to give up its entrenched dogmafication when it came to questionable religious beliefs.

We, too, have thought about retreating into solitude to achieve Self-Realization without having to deal with the negativity and close-mindedness of a sleepwalking humanity. However, we've decided to avoid what St. Augustine described as the temptation of *fuga in solitudinem* (the flight into solitude). Instead, we'll continue to openly share what we believe to be the sacred soul journey to humankind's collective enlightenment.

Quantum Exegesis

The 'Theory of Everything,' the Holy Grail of quantum physics, may always be just a 'ToE' wetting exercise in our attempt to understand the universe in which we live. We believe our quest to understand the 'nature of things'—quantum, cosmological, and psionic*—must be a combined scientifically empirical and spiritually revelatory path.

To date, the Theory of Everything doesn't pay enough attention to the psi reality of consciousness. That's why it needs to expand its bandwidth of knowledge beyond the limitations of its mathematics penchant. And I'm not the only one concerned about its built-in limitations. Here's Albert Einstein's view: "As far as the laws of mathematics refer to reality, they are not certain, and as far as they are certain, they do not refer to reality."

* Psionic means beyond the spheres of conventional physics and psychology, phantastic supersensory intelligence. The Greek letter for psi is Ψ and comes from the root word *psichy*, which means 'breath, life, soul, spirit' or the 'animating principle of mind.' As of this post, psi is the unknown extrasensory factor that modern science hasn't figured out what to do with yet.

Bad Habits

When your bad habits zig at you today, zag.

Apertured Desire Power

The achievements associated with both willpower and won't power are well-known. However, what about the implications of 'why-power' which is based on how apertured your desire power happens to be.

Your Spiritual IP Address

You can 'be' Home anytime and anywhere you want, because your Spiritual Home's IP Address is a nonlocal state of Higher Super-Consciousness. (Nonlocality doesn't have a zip code). It's been called by many names: Heaven, the Kingdom of God, Paradise, the Ph!losopher's Stone, the Promised Land, Arcadia, Nirvana, Shangri-la, Elysium, Utopia, Cosmic Consciousness, Pure Consciousness, the Field of Infinite Potential, the Garden of Eden, the Sacred City, Universal Realm, Realm of the Absolute, etc.

Here's a 'localized' example of our nonlocal reality: Identical twins, separated at birth and raised apart, nevertheless have shown striking similarities in their interests, tastes, professions, spouses and/or dating interests, entertainment preferences, and injuries, beyond what can be reasonably assumed to their common DNA. I find that fascinating, and I'm guessing you do too!

Grasping the Ungraspable

One of the highest rational achievements of the brightest of humankind is in grasping that certain things, 'logical' and intuitive, tautological and mystical, lie beyond their current intellectual powers to fully grasp—with the proviso that they can eventually be grasped.

Supersentient Transformation

I have found that in mystical insperiences, knowledge can't be separated from the extrasensory aspects of life which underwrite its manifestation. Once you acquire mystical insights you undergo quite a Supersentient transformation. I love to dabble in neuroscience and psience, evolutionary biology, and quantum physics, etc.; however, the tautology of these disciplines fails to appreciate the implications the influence of the unmanifest has on our consciousness. I believe one of the heuristics of mystical moments is that they unstiffen well-worn scientific theories.

Present Moment Catharsis

Our cathartic thoughts, intentions, choices—even our trilemma* choices—and actions are the Tao to our salvation from the limitations of our skin school experiences.

> * Trilemma choices describe situations in which a difficult choice has to be made between three equally undesirable alternatives.

Use Your Inside Voice

How many times have you heard a parent whisper to a child, "Shhhh. Use your inside voice?" How many times have you said that to your own children or grandchildren? Just prior to that warning the youngster is usually speaking at a pitch louder than is deemed necessary. The idea is you want the youngster to learn proper etiquette and accepted behavior. But the 'inside voice' we're referring to is a different kind of 'inside voice.' It's a voice we must learn to listen to when we're facing difficulties, when we suffer major setbacks, when we run into ten miles of bad road. It's a voice we must listen to if we are to grow personally and professionally. It's a voice we must pay attention to if we are to master the art of living. It's the voice that comes from what psychologists refer to as our *Authentic* or *True* Self. It's what we call your Divine Nature, the Extraordinary You! It's the 'voice of inner strength.' It's the 'Still Small Voice.' When the world is screaming its woes—when friends are letting you down — when you want to yell out in frustration and pain—when you're experiencing a dark night of the soul moment—that's when the ONLY thing to do is ... Use Your Inside Voice!

Try These on for Sighs

What do you call a 767 full of meditating mystics? An astral planc!

Have you astrally projected lately? Have you've taken friends with you? If you have, it's called mass trance-portation!

Global Allegories

The Isis and Osiri (Egypt), Persephone and Dianysus (Greece), Aphrodite and Adonis (Syria), Cybele and Attis (Asia Minor), Istar and Marduk (Mesopotamia), Magna Mater and Mithras (Persia), Asherah and Baal (Judaea), and Jesus and Mary Magdalene (an embodiment of Sophia) also Judaea, stories are the allegories of our enlightened soul growth.

Crown of Thorns

According to three of the canonical Gospels, a woven crown of thorns was placed on the head of the Christ as Jesus during his crucifixion. However, that's not the 'crown of thorns' I'm going to describe. MetaSpiritually, the 'crown of thorns' symbolizes the highly vivified and spiritualized twelve pair of cranial nerves that surround the interior of our head like a crown. When we become fully illumined they transform our perfected nervous system into a glorified body of light. This 'crown' signals our having gained conscious immortality (a halo of light). The 12 pair of cranial nerves are: olfactory, optic, motor oculi, trochlear, trifacial, abducent, facial, auditory, glosso pharyngeal, pnumogastric, spinal accessor, and hypoglossal.

Gaia Consciousness

In a fascinating experiment, researchers played the sound of a caterpillar munching on leaves to nearby plants - and the plants released defensive chemicals based on the sound alone. Isn't that incredible! Research has shown that plants have memories and even react to anesthetics. While tomatoes may not be able to scream, some plants emit compounds that warn their 'compatriots' of approaching threats - the botanical equivalent of a smoke signal. Neat huh!

The Tabula Rosa Fallacy

Our tabula rosa-ness when we're born into each human experience is an errant belief! Our embodiment in human form includes immense intellectual, extrasensory, emotional, subconscious, superconscious, etc., knowledge and experience, which are the evolutionary composite of all of our past, present, and future beingness. When we exhibit those higher sentient qualities there are many people who consider us as 'others,' as different from 'normal' people. However, this sense of 'otherness' doesn't require us to self-quarantine from 'those others' who haven't experienced extrasensory phenomena. I believe everyone has those abilities.

Gethsemane

Gethsemane is an Aramaic term (Gaḏ-Šmānê) that means 'oil press.' It's in an olive tree grove near Jerusalem. Its name derives from the process of heating nuts or seeds so you can extract natural oils. *MetaSpiritually, Gethsemane represents our struggle in skin school to align our human self with our Divine Nature. The 'oil' that we produce is our enlightenment.*

Zen There's You

The only Zen you find on silent retreats, meditation insperiences, vision quests, mountaintop experiences, Om pod session, and pandemics is the Zen you bring with you.

Our Noble Task

One of Cher and my key tasks that's associated with our MetaSpiritual perspective is to shatter false beliefs based on the hucksterism of dogmatic spin-doctors.

Dial It Up

The brain itself is dialed-up for intuitive flashes. Why? Because the synaptic connections that create intuitive highways in your neural networks are reconfigured grey matter that allows you to see things you didn't see before in a flash. Besides, intuition is simply logic in a hurry. So, dial-up your intuitive intelligence every chance you get.

Spiritual Acupuncture

What if hugs, smiles, playful eye winks, compliments, blowing kisses to each other, praying to one another's health and well-being, rest, a soothing sip of hot coffee or tea virtually shared, and mutual sharing of highly personal information are all forms of spiritual acupuncture during pandemics! Wouldn't that be evidence that there's no geography in Spirit!

Worldwide Agreement

If there was one altruistic concept that would have the biggest, most positive, lasting impact on humankind worldwide, what would it be?

Different Strokes For Different Folks

Has it ever occurred to you that something can be experienced as a different color, taste, sound, smell, or size at the same time? Here' how. When these five perceptions characterize one thing that's being seen, tasted, listened to, and smelled simultaneously by five different species, the qualities of what's being observed will most likely be experienced as different.

Our Incoming Ego and Heredity

I've come to the *wunderstanding* (that's Cher's spelling and slant on the combination of wonder and understanding) that when we come through the physical portal of an incarnation or reincarnation into our human experience we may inherit the biochemistry of our parents and their biochemical heritage, but their biochemistry is only ancillary to the karma of our having chosen that particular physical portal. Our true Soul Signature is our evolving consciousness which makes our current incoming, skin-encapsulated ego* a composite of all of our past lives and simultaneous lives in different dimensions of being. We have the psychic power to up-regulate and down-regulate the genes of our physical embodiment to achieve higher levels of health and wellness depending upon the accumulated strength and purity of our Soul Signature.

This week I discovered the quote below which predates my thinking and seems to corroborate it as well. The author, Corinne Heline, was born into the well-to-do Duke family, who were part of the Old South's aristocracy. Hers and my view about this subject are speculative, of course; however, I hope you'll find them interesting:

"While it is true that parents supply the physical atoms for building the infant body of an incoming Ego, and that a pure body cannot be provided by parents whose bodies are charged with poisons and disease, it must never be forgotten that the incarnating Ego need not remain subject to such limitations. It possesses the power to nullify every negative condition passed on to it under the Law of Heredity. It can remake its physical body atom for atom. As for the qualities of character, these are not the product of heredity or environment." (*New Birth Through Regeneration* by Corinne Heline, American author and Christian mystic)

If this post seems a little far out, it actually comes from deep within. I had read several books about karma this week and found one of Corinne's writings which triggered my entry above.

* 'Skin-encapsulated' ego was dubbed by ph!losoph!cal entertainer, Alan Watts.

Explanations Unraveled

An explanation by an authority figure is where most people rest. However, explanations—whomever and wherever they come from—should be simply considered, evaluated, perhaps modified or amended, or even dismissed.

It's About Time

Hesitation can be the longest distance between two time periods.

It'll Be a Cold Day in Hell

When you hear someone say, "It'll be a cold day in Hell"[1] before something happens, it generally means that the chances of that something happening are absolutely impossible, highly unlikely to happen, or never going to happen contrary to the ghoulish nature of this fictional religious Gehenna. The operative sentiment is: it's NEVER going to happen!

The other two idioms similar to 'a cold day in hell' that express the same sentiments are: 'When hell freezes over,' and 'Not a snowball's chance in hell.' A more recent 'hellish' idiom goes something like this, 'Hell doesn't have air-conditioning.'

What's interesting about all of these 'cold day in hell' sentiments is that they all imply that 'hell' is a place, a place regarded in many dogmatically-inclined religious traditions as the realm of evil and everlasting punishment and suffering for sinners. This dogmatic 'place' drips with flapdoodleness.[2]

The original 'cold day in hell' idiomatic expression is believed to have originated sometime in the late 19th century in America, perhaps around 1888 or 1889. Its etymology is 'cold natured' so etymologists haven't gotten warm enough to pinpoint its origins.

Here's the thing—because we believe hell is merely a state of fractured consciousness (a hellish one, we might add) that can be described as a state of mind that retails suffering, torment and anguish, misery, and wickedness, hatefulness and violence, denial of our innate divinity, and deceitfulness and disrespect for others—we can cool off those divisive thoughts and hellish !ncl!nat!ons, because hell is *heir conditioned*! It always has been '*heir conditioned*' because we're heir to our thoughts, intentions, choices and actions whether they're Self-affirming/self-affirming or Self-negating/self-negating.[3]

Sooo, look at a hellish state of consciousness this way when it comes to your reaction to Covid-19—use your 'heir power' to stay cool, calm and collected so you can stay 'heir conditioned' through, and beyond, this viral threat. Affirm your health and wellness and the health and wellness of everyone on the planet—as you wash your hands of the virus, avoid mask confusion, and keep a safe distance from it!

[1]As a side note, it's a fact that Hell — which is between Flint and Ann Arbor, Michigan — actually froze over in 2004 and again on Jan. 7, 2014. (There's also a Hell, California located near Interstate 10 which was built in 1964 and founded 10 years earlier in 1954 by Charles Carr.

[2]Flapdoodleness refers to people who are prey to foolishness, indigestible dogmatic nonsense, irrationality, harebrained ideas, absurdity, short-sightedness, etc.

[3]Self-affirming/self-affirming or Self-negating/self-negating refers to our capital 'S' Divine Self and our small 's' human self.

Let It Sync In

Allow the cosmic twinship of your Human Nature and your Divine Nature to sync in!

Creating NèW noRmÅls

Usually, and we're sure you've experienced this, what you wish for when it comes to handling unexpected 'NèW noRmÅls,' doesn't tend to fall into your lap easily! Sound familiar! The challenges a 'NèW noRmÅl' presents usually fall somewhere outside your comfort zone, allowing you opportunities to incorporate them into your life easier— and/or it means stretching your patience, talents, and resources to accommodate the changes it poses.

Sooo, when it comes to living happily and healthily, why not see 'old normals' and some of the 'NèW noRmÅls' as 'both ands' and not 'either ors.'

Neuro-Communions

Mystical moments and meditation are neuro-communions with our Omnipresent Universal Realityness.

Your Cellular Family Is Listening

Cher and I invite you to fully resonate with this statement: your cells, atoms, and molecules are conscious cellular beings. They know when you have their best interests in mind. So, take care of your cellular family … because your cells are always listening to your thoughts … they're always the beneficiaries of each choice you make … they always have to process what you eat and drink … and the actions you take always affect their well-being.

Your cellular family is a living, evolving, adapting bioverse, which uses information to organize itself and to create ever-increasing levels of complexity. That makes your physical body more verb than noun. By that we mean your cellular architecture, emotionality, sense of self, and mental functioning have four-way conversations 24-7-365… supporting each other toward ensuring your—and their—continued wellness.

The Prism of Positivity

The *prism* of positivity's light-generating capacity sees the *prison* of negativity's darkness as only a speed bump, not a holding cell. Optimistic people know this. That's why they brush off negativity like lint off their clothing. So, practice 'lint removal' every chance you get.

Information and Outformation

The mind-bending expansive nature of my mystical moments has shown me that accumulated knowledge is merely a *process* of information acquisition and not a static *product* to be dogmatized. *Information* is only as good as the *outformation* it generates. Knowledge is more verb than noun.

Quantumplating

When you think about it, contemplating on the nature of Omnipresent Universal Reality from a panoptic quantum physics perspective is really *quantumplating* on the nature of Omnipresent Universal Reality.

A Consciousness Triage

Recognize that until humankind collectively moves toward that universal symbiosis of enlightened thought that illumined outliers have described, humankind's collective journey in skin school is one in need of a serious higher consciousness triage.

The Apostrophe Effect

If you take the word *Impossible* and place an apostrophe between the I and the m and leave a space after the m, you get *I'm possible*!

Unintelligent Design

There are those (religious fundamentalists and creationists) who champion the belief in the intelligent design orchestrated by an omnipotent, omniscient, omnipresent Grand Designer. And there are those (evolutionary biologists and anatomists, geologists, evolutionists, cosmologists, biogeographists, quantum physicists, ecologists, exobiologists* (also astrobiologists), and people, in general, who have common sense, to name a few) who trust in evidence-based science and psience over blind belief.

The following observation should settle the debate once and for all from a common sensical viewpoint: The historical and modern day pattern of billions of gazillions of major design flaws, unfortunate mistakes, obvious 'back to the drawing board' structural dilemmas, catastrophic imperfections, horrendous ad hoc modifications, botched environmental architecture, constant format and construction tweaking and tinkering, endless rejiggering, warranty claims filed on defective systems and life forms, etc.—all point to unintelligent design!

You may even have to concede, if you're a Grand Designer fan, that there must have been a phenomenal rush job involved on the sixth day of creation that left much to be desired in terms of the considerable lack of quality evident in the over-all nature of creation.

*Exobiologists (also astrobiologists) is the study of the possibility of interstellar extraterrestrial life).

Our MetaSpiritual Perspective

Cher's and my MetaSpiritual perspective champions the marriage between evidence-based science, experient-based psience, faith-based spirituality, and metaphor-based

43

metaphysics. In other words, we've placed the Trojan Horses of science and spirituality in the Troy of mainstream religion.

Rediculate

As Cher and I've listened to the national news in 2020-2021, I came up with a word to describe how pompous some people sound when they spread disinformation, misinformation, and other falsehoods. The word I coined was: *rediculate*! Here's an example of using 'rediculate' in a sentence: Rediculators who spread false information, bogus beliefs, and purposefully plant obnoxious rumors to influence public opinion is to rediculate the spread of falsehoods. Forgive me, but I can't help seeing Pinocchio's proboscis lie detector on their faces as they're retailing their falsehoods.

Troglodyte Blindness

You've probably heard of Plato's Cave Analogy. He suggested that we're all trapped inside of a cave and know the world only through the shadows that are cast on the wall by the movements of the troglodyte occupants who are blinded by the darkness they've adopted. Interestingly, our skull is our 'cave,' and our ingrained blind suppositions, beliefs, complacency, and biases are our shadows.

*Troglodyte refers to a human being cave dweller or one who inhabits the area beneath the overhanging rocks of a cliff.

YOUniversal Prosperity

Our YOUniversal prosperity message is a departure from the impediment of depending on a primitive anthropomorphic god meme for our greater good. Recognize that you're a highly conscious expression of the Omnipresent Universal Reality actualizing as you in human form. Don't doubt for a moment, that you're that Omnipresent Universal Reality becoming aware of your Universal Beingness through the filters of your human experience in skin school!

Less Than Philosophical

Whenever I find myself less than philosophical, I attribute it to a momentary lapse of Riesling.

Gapping Gaps

It's apparent to me that psiology* has filled in the gaps that brute scientism, with its statistical mundanity, has left empty. It seems that scientism's closed-mindedness has them by the scruff of their collective necks.

*Psiology is the study of psi abilities.

Teleology vs Nonteleology

Darwin and Wallace's evolutionary natural selection reduced 'theological teleology into nonteleology (Grand Design into Non-anthropomorphic Order).

Uncorking

Mystical moments help us uncork the mental blockage that hides our True Higher Consciousness Identity: we are the Omnipresent Universal Reality actualizing as us in human form!

Libations

Spiritual practices, spiritually-attuned thoughts and feelings, compassion, and forgiveness are 'higher consciousness libations' offered to our continued soul growth.

Manifesting Your Greater Good

Understand and wisely use the basic manifestation principles associated with the various skin school environments you're in, as well as their inter-relationships. This manifestation principle is KEY to manifesting your Greater Good! It underwrites the whole manifestation process! The environments we're talking about are: health, wealth, interpersonal, cultural, material, occupational, spiritual, etc., to name a few. And remember—here's our cautionary proviso— you can use these principles for self-interest and/or Self-interest!

Ph!losoph!cally Wandering

Time spent ph!losoph!cally wandering is never wasted.

Between the Lines

The main message in all of Cher's and my books and writings is: Because our carbon-based rainbow bodies are simply lower vibrations of the Omnipresent Universal Reality, the real stuff in written words is in the blank spaces between the lines where what you'll read generates your own spiritual unfoldment and raises your vibration to Super-Conscious levels of unfoldment.

Crystal Methology

Indigestible, toilsome dogma is the crystal meth of fundamentalist religion's bafflegab. It hooks you quickly and kills your factual nature even faster.

Enjoy Your Skin School Experience

To truly encounter the human experience—or to encounter any other physical dimension of beingness—means to experience the wonder and exhilaration and mysteries of it that bring us incredible joy and happiness. So, enjoy your skin school experience for its soul growth value. It's the current version of you. It's the you that's the author of your current unfoldment, an unfoldment that can be the catalyst of your eventual Self-Realization.

A Velcroed Bias

Religious fundamentalism sticks like Velcro to evidence-barren, hyperdogmatic beliefs and slides off evidenced-based truths like Teflon.

Unselfing

One of my ph!losoph!cal !ncl!nat!ons took me here: Spiritual growth is an 'unselfing' from an unenlightened ego and lifelong negative patterns in the subconscious. In the spiritually-minded this process is raised to the 'nth' degree of intensity. It means passionately seeking your Absoluteness, your Higher Spiritual Essence, the longing for your alignment with your Life Force, for understanding who you really are as a highly super-conscious being. Those who move beyond unenlightened egocentric antics, have already separated themselves from tons of karmic baggage.

Our Collective Behavior

If the human species doesn't still exist 500 years from now, it'll most likely be because we haven't pruned materialism, racism, anthropomorphic god-ism, misogyny, prejudice, hypocrisy, exclusivity, etc., from our collective behavior.

Life Sentience

If we're in the physical world, but not of the physical world, which I believe is true, science—with all of its researched 'factual' information based on observational statistics, hasn't been able to enter our 'other world,' the subjective consciousness realm. It seems as if science's current worldview is a 'life sentience' without parole!

Supersentient Mosaics

We are spectacular Supersentient mosaics woven together by our unitive consciousness and karma.

Namasté-ing Around

After one of my meditations, I closed by saying 'Shalom.' Sometimes I simply say 'OM' three times, other times I've said 'Namasté,' and still other times I've said 'Moksha.' However, on this occasion, after saying 'Shalom,' which is a highly spiritual greeting that means 'peace,' it occurred to me that 'Shalom' is most certainly an appropriate greeting when you live in troubled times. And, unfortunately, we live in troubled times. Then, it also occurred to me that meditation and mystical experiences are a higher form of connection with the truth of who and what I really am; higher say, than affirming that cosmic connection and higher than merely reading and studying about higher truths.

Being peaceful, loving, compassionate, kindhearted, altruistic, respectful, courteous, etc., are all polite forms of interpersonal connection based on civility. And I thoroughly support those qualities. However, it occurred to me that there may be a more universal greeting which is more comprehensive and all-inclusive in nature—'Namasté.' It means 'I bow to your true nature' or 'I bow to your true divine nature.' To me, it's a perfect salutation. It champions our True Eternal Nature which is an individualized Life Force of the Omnipresent Universal Reality actualized as us in human form.

So, I begin my spiritual practices with OM and conclude them with Namasté. I invite you to do something similar which celebrates your Timeless Divine Status.

Embodiment

I've found that there's something much more powerful than simply clarifying your ph!losophy. It's embodying it!

Attending the 'C' Word—Church

No matter how you look at it, going to church every week doesn't make you a Christian (Jew, Buddhist, Hindu, Baha'i, Catholic, etc.) any more than standing in your garage makes you a car, SUV, truck or motorcycle! You've got to put your beliefs into practice!

Couple of Good Swift Kicks

Has it occurred to you that if you could give the person who's the most responsible for your troubles a couple of good swift kicks, *you* wouldn't be able to sit down for a week?

Brain Meme's Point of View

One of the arguments for assuming that the brain produces consciousness is that, if the brain is damaged, consciousness has to be impaired or altered. However, this is a brain meme's point of view that's based on the premise that consciousness is a product (secretion, leakage) of the brain. That doesn't make sense if you believe—as I do—that the brain simply receives, records and transmits conscious impulses, leaving neuronal footprints of consciousness.

I speculate that our brain acts as a kind of neural antenna that interacts with our mind as an external conduit of the non-anthropomorphic Omnipresent Universal Reality. Here's a quick analogy: a radio doesn't produce the music that comes through it, and if it's damaged, its ability to transmit music will be impaired or stopped altogether. However, other radios, unaffected by that radio's demise, are still transmitting music, news, and other programming.

Higher Consciousness Refuges

Anomalous experiences like mystical moments, precognitive dreams, ordinary dreams, déjà vu experiences, and trance states, are higher consciousness refuges against conventional thinking and mind-numbing habits that cling to long-standing fictions rather than embrace obvious truths.

Multiversed

Because our universe was most likely 'birthed' by a precursor Multiverse, you could say we're 'multiversed' in our understanding of who we are and where we've come from—we speak ufology, string theory, brane theory, Big Bang theory, the Big Bounce theory, Bubble Universe theory, theological banter, philosophical chitchat, and so on.

Sooo, is our universe a string'ed universe, a bran'ed universe, Big Bang'ed universe, a Big Bounc'ed universe, or a Bubbl'ed universe? Check out our White Light Paper entitled: *What Existed Before Our Big Bang—Or When Did Time Itself Begin?*)

They're No Match

My iPad has beaten me at WGT Golf, and my Apple laptop beats me at solitaire, but they're no match for me at frisbee golf or horseshoes.

Quantumverse Vernacular

Everything we see in physicality (our carbon-based bodies, our thoughts and feelings, tables and chairs, coffee pots, tress, animals and insects, the sun and planets, solar systems, this book you're reading, etc.) is a form of 'quantumverse vernacular' (the language of the universe's collapsed wave function).

Cloistered Enlightenment

Think of it like this. Mystical moments are cloistered glimpses into enlightenment for those who have inner eyes to see, the !ncl!nat!on and patience to capture Aha's, and the soulfulness to intuitively grasp transcendental truths and realities. It means moving from the limitations of the semi-conscious you (the dogmatically hyper-religious-oriented you) to the liberated Super-Conscious you (the you that unhesitatingly explores the farther reaches of Satoric wisdom).

Doorway Threshold Effect

We've all done it. Walk upstairs to get your keys, but forget that it's the keys you're looking for once you get to the bedroom. Open the fridge door and reach for the middle shelf only to realize that you can't remember why you opened the fridge in the first place. Or wait for a moment to interrupt a friend to find that the burning issue that made us want to interrupt has now vanished from your mind just as you come to speak: "What did I want to say again?"

Although these episodes can be embarrassing, they're also common. They're known as the 'Doorway Threshold Effect,' and they reveal some important features of how our minds are organized. The Doorway Effect occurs because we change both the physical and mental environments by moving to a different room and thinking about different things. That hastily thought up goal (getting the keys or reaching for something on the middle shelf in the fridge, are merely contextual thoughts among the many thoughts we're spinning at that moment, and our original intention gets lost when the context changes. Of course, carrying your bride across the threshold falls under a whole different context and is a whole different matter. I'm just sayin'.

Brain Hemispheric Synchronization and Accelerated Enlightenment

A 2012 UCLA School of Medicine study found that the corpus callosum, the grand central station-like cable of nerves cross-linking our brain hemispheres, is remarkably stronger, thicker, and more well connected in meditation practitioners.

For those looking to maximize their cognitive potential, what does this monumental neuroplastic healthy brain discovery mean? By constructing a hyper-connected, ultra-efficient bridge between our brain hemispheres, meditation puts an abrupt end to our 'Neuro-Cold-War, by synchronizing our 'east' and 'west' brain hemispheres.

Synchronizing both brain hemispheres opens the door to a smorgasbord of cerebral benefits, with better focus, deeper thought, super creativity, excellent mental health, the enhanced embroidery of memory, clearer thinking—and wait for this—accelerated enlightenment! There's no need for drug-assisted 'highs.' Actually, there's never been a need for artificial 'highs.' We can get there through Brain Hemispheric Synchronization meditational experiences. (To find out more about that, check out our White Light Paper entitled *Mental Ping Pong: Brain Hemispheric Synchronization.*)

The Path of Least Insistence

Realize that processed foods generally extend both their shelf life and your waistline. The extra unwanted pounds and inches we add are generally caused by the 'path of least insistence'—neglecting to 'insist' on eating healthily.

Great Truths

Great truths need to be intellectually and figuratively simonized not idolized!

Contentment Personified

If you can breathe easily after hearing upsetting news; if you can happily consume whatever's placed on your dinner plate; if, in downturns in the economy, you remain absolutely cool, calm, and collected; if you notice that your next door neighbor has purchased a new luxury vehicle without feeling a bit of resentment; if you can relax after an extremely eventful day without a beer or a pill; if you can fall asleep watching TV without feeling guilty; if you get high-spirited when the kids want you to play—you're probably contented with your enlightened you-ness!

Be Wary of the Cartel of Ignorance

Divinity-denying thoughts, anti-spiritual words and choices, and self-aggrandizing actions are the unenlightened ego's pathological cartel of ignorance.

Evidence-Based or Evidence-Barren

To say that current sciences and current dogmatic religions espouse ultimate truths is simply to say that their renditions of truths are merely epistemological beliefs about truths, awaiting more evidence of validation or contradictory evidence. BUT, and it's a very big BUT, evidence-barren dogmas are a propensity toward 'darkness' that our unenlightened ego prefers, because as the lyrics in the Phantom of the Opera song, The Music of the Night, remind us: "In the dark, it is easy to pretend."

Feng Shuied Thinking

An impure thought usually leads to a tainted choice and/or action. And to extend the analogy, an immoral choice generally leads to an unethical consequence. It is best, of course, to 'Feng Shui' our thinking so our thinking leads to the right choices and actions. And that implies living from a spiritual perspective so our actions are consistent with our professed beliefs and values.

Parapsi-chiatry's Clarity

Hallucinations are generally regarded as 'abnormal by traditional psychiatrists except when these episodes occur during certain physiologically heightened states of consciousness like sleep-onset (hypnagogic) moments, awakening out-of-sleep (hypnopompic) moments, and lucid dreaming moments. (See my Psi-Favorable Environments post).

Pavlov's Dogs and Schrodinger's Cat

I read somewhere that a customer walked into a bookstore and asked if they carried a book about Pavlov's dogs and Schrodinger's cat in the science section. The clerk said, "It rings a bell, but I don't know if it's there or not!"

Present Moments

Pause just for a moment and think about this - present moments never come to an end. That's the nature of Present Moment Reality.

A Mind Phenomenon

Psi is a mind phenomenon; and a theory of psi, then, needs to be coupled with a theory of mind to understand Consciousness. Just as the mind is a subjective experience of Universal Consciousness, the brain is a subjective experience of mind.

Abiogenesis-izing

The incredible complexity of the simplest cellular life forms is sooo awesome that it's hard to imagine that such primordial sentient life forms on Earth (and other planets) could have suddenly appeared from spontaneous generation unless they may have been the products of exoterrestrial and panspermian influences. We don't what was in the prebiotic, alchemicalized, quantum soup.

I love putting jigsaw puzzles together. However, I don't have time, nor the !ncl!nat!on, to piece these puzzles together simply by shaking the pieces! However, if I thought these jigsaws had sentience, I'd love to watch their abiogenesis-izing into more complex puzzle pieces to see what they could co-create.

Metagapism

The theological perspective of 'God of the gaps' is an irrational perspective that proselytizes that science can't explain 'gaps' in religious beliefs which are filled with nonfalsifiable dogmatic bloating to describe God's intervention in human affairs. Sooo, *metagapism* is a belief that I consider open to interpretation. I see it as 'meta' (going beyond) the 'God of the gaps' religious argument mentioned above: When something is 'nonfalsifiable' it can't be proven to be absolutely true or definitively false, even if science has poked enough holes in the argument to indicate the gap's replicability hasn't been proven and the so called 'gap' is most likely a false claim to the satisfaction of the 'God of the gaps' holders!

The Call to Higher Consciousness Citizenship

All mystics, write those who study heightened paranormal abilities, speak the same language and come from the same 'country.' Mystics agree that the most important goal for humankind is to see more deeply into what is, to go considerably beyond ordinary perceptions, and to fully comprehend and experience rather than just understand the Greater Realities.

Mystics, they say, agree that there's two basic states of consciousness: the normal, lower vibrational everyday state of awareness, and the other is the higher vibrational Way of Oneness, because there's only undivided wholeness. This one-ing with our One Realityness is a call to higher consciousness planetary and cosmic citizenship, with landing gears in the lower consciousness realm as well.

Mystical moments are soul-charging higher consciousness events. Unitary mystical moments and other psioneering experiences aren't fleeting extrasensory binges whose purpose is to disrupt ordinary states of consciousness. They free us from the shackles of lower vibrational clock time and send us, straightjacket-free to realms of a higher order of limitless cosmic beingness. The extrasensory punch and paranormal vigor must become part of humankind's legitimate and accepted 21st century reality consensus.

Ontological !ncl!nat!ons

Perhaps humankind's ultimate ph!losoph!cal challenge is to discover the ontology of the Omnipresent Universal Reality.

Zenfulness

The evolutionary process seems to be gradualistic with periods of stasis (relatively slowed adaptation), where each new generation is slightly different and only slightly more complex than its previous generation. There's something verrry Zen about that!

'Heard' Immunity

During the Covid-19 Pandemic of 2020-2021, 'Herd Immunity' (population immunity) is achieved when a large enough portion (95%) of a community (the herd) is immune to a virus so that the virus can no longer spread easily from person to person. As a result, the entire community is protected, even those who aren't themselves immune yet. Herd immunity is usually achieved through vaccination, which is the preferred intervention, but it can also occur through natural infection.

By analogy, 'Heard Immunity' is a spiritual concept which refers to humankind as a whole (the herd) who've 'heard' about their Divine Genealogy and use that spiritual Truth as an immunity from the disastrous consequences of believing in a primitive anthropomorphic god meme that retails fear, guilt and shame to control the gullible faithful.

Vegetarian Lions?

Expecting some 'breeds' of people to treat you non-pejoratively because you're a good person is like expecting a hungry lion not to attack you because you're an avowed vegetarian.

Linear Stagnation

Forward-thinking, panoptic, MetaSpiritual perspectives will bring us exponential soul growth while puffed-up dogmatic religious beliefs with a whiff of flapdoodleness (what I call dogmatic bloating) will continue to soil us with their flummoxed ideologies and linear stagnation. The thing about misinformation-guided dogmas, nonsensical paradigms, and confirmation biases, is that the people retailing those disinformation ideologies will not hesitate to pee on your leg and tell you it's raining.

Our Sentience and Supersentience

Sentience means self-awareness, especially feelings and sensations based on self-consciousness. Supersentience refers to higher Self-Awareness and Self-Consciousness that feature extrasensory qualities that more fully connect us with our Divine Nature. The word, sentience, was first coined by philosophers in the 1630s to refer to the ability to feel, derived from Latin sentientem (a feeling).

How Many You's Are There?

Philosophers and spiritual leaders call it your Divine Nature, your Transcendent Self. It's the you we call the Extraordinary You, your Supersentient Self. So, let's talk about you - the Intuitively Wise You, the Spectacular You, the Spiritual You, the MetaSpiritual You, the Authentic You, the Phenomenal You, the Peerless You, the Exceptional You, the Unparalleled You, the Legendary You, the Marvelous You, the One-of-a-Kind You, the Remarkable You, the Awesome You, the Prosperous You, the Amazing You, the Astounding You, the Electrifying You, the Stunning You, the Sensational You, the Mesmerizing You, the Spellbinding You, the Hypnotic You, the Metaphysical You, the Fascinating You, the Mystical You, the Fantabulous You, the Mediumship You, the Brilliant You, the Super You, the Stupendous You, the Jaw-Dropping You, the Mind-Blowing You, the Spiritualist You, the Scientific You, Compassionate You, the Philanthropic You, the Loving You, the Joyful You, the Thoughtful You, the

Philosophical You, the Perceptive You, the Creative You, the Blissful You, the Beautiful You, the Self-Aware You, the Optimistic You, the Soulful You, the Self-Realized You, the Überconscious You, the Transhuman You, the Extrasensory You, the Supersentient You, the Non-Dogmatic You, the Posthuman You, the You Who Questions Unquestioned Answers, and millions more positive You's!

If it sounds like I'm going overboard with those positive descriptions of you, I invite you to recognize how incredible you are as a spiritual being having a human experience.

Knowing Yourself and 'No-ing' Yourself

It occurs to me that knowing yourself also means "no-ing" yourself - you know, saying 'no' to your fears, doubts, feelings of unworthiness, etc. We're all rare, complicated, and all-too-delicate organisms wrapped in our own particular packages of DNA. The speck of consciousness which becomes us bursts into personhood, remains for a time, then vanishes again as we 'graduate' from our human experience, and soar to our next adventure in consciousness. So don't waste precious time looking outside yourself to find your Self.

Wallowing in Confusion

Those who don't jump out of their dogmatic boxes have decided to continue to wallow in their confusion.

Naturally !ncl!ned

In college and graduate school I majored in transpersonal psychology and ph!losophy with strong !ncl!nat!ons toward spirituality and mysticism.

The Omnipresent You

Wherever you go, whenever you go, however you go, whyever you go, whichever you go—there you are!

Beyond Mere Sentience

I've got to tell you, at the risk of being ostracized by the fundamentalist community, that confronting the stale religious status quo and presenting our own radically different spiritual perspective of life means embracing a higher form of Supersentience. Cher's and my unquenchable thirst for the truth has led us to challenge evidence-barren beliefs of all kinds of religious, scientific, educational, health-related, etc., persuasions.

Turning Surge Capacity Into Surge Protection

I've mentioned the proverbial 'calm and connect response,' the 'connect and bonding response,' and the 'fight-flight-freeze-please response' in My Mystical Moment Musings book, which all relate to turning surge capacity into surge protection. I'd like to expand those three adaptive and survival schemes as they relate to this post.

It involves the concept of 'surge capacity' developed by psychologist, Ann Masten, PhD. As she describes it, 'surge capacity' is a collection of adaptive systems (mental and emotional) that we humans draw on for short-term survival in acutely stressful situations, such as natural disasters, global catastrophes, pandemics, etc. The questions become: What do you do when your 'surge capacity' is depleted and the new normal isn't anywhere in sight? What happens when your personal operating system is out of options?

All of these sometimes frightening scenarios (surges) that are generated by the world outer appearances, can deplete your surge capacity, your ability to handle that kind of stress, especially if it's long term. However, if your personal operating system includes a highly spiritual aspect, you can turn your over-all surge capacity into surge protection! If you haven't already, make cutting edge spiritual practices your 'new normal' - that is, your escape velocity from depleted surge capacity!

You have complete control over how your respond to the world of outer experiences. Aligning your human nature with your Divine Nature is the perfect 'surge protection' you'll need while you're matriculating through skin school.

Hard Wired or Wi-Fied?

As I wrote these posts I wondered what readers' responses would be if I could sit with them for a brief moment and ask: Do you feel hard-wired or Wi-Fied to your Divine Nature?

Inbreath-Ogenesis

Our inbreath is life starting over, one breath at a time.

The Big Bang

I'm going to use our universe's storied 'big bang' as an analogy for what goes on in our mind. The 'big bang' in highly spiritual terms is the creation of a thought or idea in the prism of our mind. Once an idea has exploded into conscious awareness it creates energy as an expression of that explosive cognitive moment. The energy it creates leads to other explosive moments (the formation of thoughts and intentions).

These super-heated moments (thought formation) expand into ideas that expand (neuroplastic inflation) into beliefs (galaxies) which in turn expand into choices that lead to physical actions. Each thought (big bang) is the outgrowth of our psycho-emotional make-up with its clusters and super-clusters of past experiences, patterns of behavior and habits, hang-ups, memories, and personal beliefs and prejudices.

Our consciousness (multiverse) is composed of our core beliefs (planets, stars, and galaxies), values (light), thoughts (particles), !nclinat!ons (quantum fluctuations), and emotional hang-ups (entropy) that lead to a personal philosophy that defines the limits of our over-all growth (expansion). We'll be able to universe hop and multiverse hop any time we want.

The Speed of Light

If you're traveling in your Mercedes convertible going at the speed of light, what happens when you turn on the headlights?

GOMU

GOMU is the acronym Cher and I use for 'God Of My Understanding.' We encourage members of our spiritual community to define what the God of their understanding is! Then we invite them to ask themselves: How do my beliefs about GOMU contribute to my YOUniversal Prosperity*?

> *YOUniversal Prosperity is the alignment of your human nature with your Divine Nature so you can experience the highest, most elevated levels of health, happiness, inner peace and financial freedom.

Chalice of Eternal Enlightenment

Our higher consciousness neuroverse is a limitless, ceilingless, chalice, a borderless container of eternal enlightenment.

Evolutionary Evolveability

It has long been proselytized by religious fundamentalists and human-centric cultures, in general, that nature and creation itself is specifically here for humankind's benefit. I call your attention to Genesis 1:26 in the Judeo-Christian Bible which says explicitly:

Then God said, "Let us make mankind in our image, in our likeness, so that they may rule over the fish in the sea and the birds in the sky, over the livestock and all the wild animals, and over all the creatures that move along the ground."

This narcissistic pronouncement pervaded humankind's primordial eccentricity 1 million years ago, 10,000 years ago, during medieval Christendom, and is the prevalent attitude worldwide today.

However, what if the Genesis account got it all wrong? What if all of the fish, fowl in the sky, animals—and Gaia herself—aren't here for the sole purpose of pleasing us humans? What if they're simply here as a result of the gradual evolveability into what they've become, as of this post, and of what they'll become as they continue to evolve? And that evolveability scenario applies to us, as well!

Life on Earth evolved from simple-to-complex, nonsentient-to-sentient because our blue speck in the cosmos is considered what astronomers and astrobiologists call a 'Goldilocks' planet.* Soooo, life—all life, including our own—was birthed by gradual evolutionary simplification-to-complexification, nonsentience-to-sentience process. Billions of bacteria, plants, insects, fish, and animals have evolved before us, and their myriad thriveability is due to their adaptation to the changing environment. And our thriveability, as well, is due to our adaptation to Earth's constant environmental changeability.

Every living thing's adaptation response is written in its DNA—including ours! Think about it! Living things want to go on living! And how they—we—accomplish that is to be able to reproduce our particular species. It's sort of an evolutionary 'duplicate me'—'copy me'—'replicate me' natural selection process. Every living thing evolves characteristics that help ensure its sustainability, survivability, and thriveability. Isn't that cool!

Our having dominion over fish, the fowl of the sky, animals—and I'm going to include plants and Gaia, in general—is missing the point entirely. I reiterate, we evolve alongside of everything else with the same DNA-driven duplicability and replication program for survival and thriveability.

A better interpretation of the Genesis passage above is a MetaSpiritual one. It promotes not only our husbandry of the planet, but the husbandry of our personal qualities: The bacteria, viruses, single-celled micro-organisms, fish, insects, reptiles, fowl of the air, animals, etc., all represent qualities, characteristics, habits, life patterns, biases, beliefs, etc., within us! Soooo, of course, we have dominion (control, sovereignty, power, mastery, authority, etc.) over all of those personality traits! We get to duplicate our better qualities for our continued health, happiness and survival, or we can replicate our self-defeating patterns that can lead to dissatisfaction, personal and global conflict, and species extinction. Our evolveability is up to us!

*A Goldilocks planet and/or Goldilocks Zone, is a circumstellar habitable zone and is within the range of orbits around a star within which a planetary surface can support liquid water given sufficient atmospheric pressure, which are key ingredients for inhabitable life. By the way, Proxima Centauri b is an exoplanet orbiting in the habitable zone of the red dwarf star Proxima Centauri, which is the closest star to the Sun and part of its triple star system. At just four light-years, it's by far the closest Earth-like planet we know about.

Existential Filibusters

It occurs to me that ph!losophers may very well be existential filibusters.

Neurons Firing

No matter how closely neuroscientists stare at a CT scan or fMRI of the human brain, the 'hot spots' that light up in our grey matter won't tell them much about what's in the subjective experience of the meditator, or quantum physicist, or metaphysicist they're examining. There's much more to consciousness than neurons simply firing!

Rational Lies

A perspective is like a brick. It can be used to benefit one's self and the greater good of others. Or it can be thrown through a window to shatter clarity and fair play.

Somatic Apprenticeship

Know that your earth life is but one school of unfoldment. It's 'skin school.' It's a somatic apprenticeship. It's an inning not an ending. It's you fancying your soul growth. Be absolutely clear about this, your human body is a garment you wear to clothe your choice to become the physical being that you are. It's your biological address. It's the 'somatic spacetime suit' you've constructed to house your particular version of Spirit.

Understand that your matriculation through different states of consciousness, in different dimensions of being, in rented vehicles (physical bodies), and in different spacetime continuums, is a journey you've chosen to make on your way toward the Self-Realization that comes from attaining full and complete Selfhood (your complete conscious One-ing with Omnipresent Universal Reality).

Shared Gullibility

It's occurred to me to ask: What's the gullibility difference in touting a non-existent primitive anthropomorphic male God meme or its non-existent anthropomorphic female God counterpart?

68

Are You In-to-It?

After one of my sitting meditation sessions, I decided to caboose it with a meditative walk. Ten minutes or so into my walk, I had the following insight which prompted me to interrupt the walk long enough to jot the insight down: When you intuit something you're really *'in-to-it'*— you know, at a deeper level of knowing that by-passes the slower rational mind's linear reasoning process. Enjoy *'in-to-iting'* as a regular cutting-edge spiritual practice.

Fallible Infallibility

As far as I know, the teachings of the Buddhist religious tradition are meant to be eternal; however, even the Buddha didn't proclaim their infallibility.

Raising Our Are-ness

It's no doubt clear to you by now that raising our Consciousness requires raising our Are-ness to reach our Is-ness! Just like our brain merely records and registers what our mind sends to it, we must simply raise our awareness, receptivity and energy at the human level (our Are-ness) in order to express our Pure Universal Consciousness Nature (our Isness).

The Eternal Presence

We're the Eternal Presence 'outposted' as us in human form.

Does Free Will Really Exist?

More than 20 years ago the American brain scientist Benjamin Libet found a brain signal, the so-called "readiness-potential" that occurred a fraction of a second before a conscious decision. Libet's experiments sparked a huge debate. Many scientists argued that if our decisions are prepared subconsciously by the brain, then our feeling of "free will" must be an illusion.

Research has found that it's the subconscious brain that makes our decisions, not our conscious mind. Subsequent research by John-Dylan Haynes and many others now show that subconscious brain activity predicts - even up to 7 seconds ahead of time - how we decide anything. The work calls into question the 'consciousness' of our decisions and may even challenge ideas about how 'free' we are to make a choice at a particular point in time.

Soulful Contentment

Contentment is soulful wealth. Luxurious living can be artificial contentedness.

Our Absolutized Beingness

Although we're still Absolutized in our human beingness in skin school, we're operating at a lower level of vibrational sentience than we'll be 100 years from now, and certainly 1,000 years from then. Of course, it'll require us to recognize our eternality as the Omnipresent Universal Reality actualizing as us in human form.

What Happens in Vagus

Did you know that your vagus nerve, along with its neuropeptide partner, oxytocin, is responsible for the *calm-and-connect response* that's every bit as ingrained evolutionarily as your *fight-flight and freeze response*. And it's been around just as long as the *fight-flight and freeze response.*

We are biologically endowed with the ability to cope with change—any amount and intensity of change—even when that change is perceived as stressful. The *calm and connection response* is associated with trust, self-reliance and curiosity instead of fear, anger and helplessness. Our bodies are pharmacies of health and wellness!

Blissing Out

Blissing out means going within to find the nirvanic you, the transcendental you, the supernatural you, the extrasensory you, the Supersentient you, the Superconscious you, the time traveler you, the neuro-versatile you, the Self-Realized you, the future you, the exo-terrestrial you, and so on.

Writer's Itch

When it comes to a writer's itch, even in long periods of solitude, loneliness nor boredom exists.

Affirmative Prayer and Brain Power

Deep parts of our brain are involved in affirmative prayer: the medial prefrontal cortex and the posterior cingulate cortex. These parts of the brain are involved in self-reflection and self-soothing.

Affirmative prayer moves us away from the fight, flight and freeze responses of the amygdala which shuts down our executive functioning (which is in the prefrontal cortex) and prevents us from thinking clearly.

Affirmative prayer triggers the release of a happy DOSE of neuro-chemicals: dopamine, oxytocin, serotonin and endorphins, which are the feel good neuro-chemicals that give us a good feeling despite facing threats like pandemics. Dopamine is the chemical that helps us anticipate happiness, oxytocin helps us feel empathy for others going through the same trauma, serotonin lifts our mood, and endorphins help us power through discomfort and fear.

DVD'ed or Synapsed?

Just as a DVD (form) isn't the movie (content) it contains, our brain (form) isn't the emotions or thoughts (content) it registers.

Bodies In Motion

Bodies in motion tend to stay in motion, and bodies at rest tend to stay napping in bed unless their parents encourage them to get up for school.

Our Choices Seem to Be Influenced Choices and Not Free Choices

One significant finding is that our brain seems to commit to certain decisions before we become aware of having made them. Research suggests that our conscious self doesn't initiate all behavior. Instead, the conscious self is somehow alerted to a given behavior that the rest of the brain and body are already planning and performing. (Libet, Gleason, Wright and Pearl, Brain, 1983, 106 [Pt3]:623-642).

Neuroscientists tell us that there's a time delay in the time it takes information out in the world to reach our conscious awareness—a nanosecond delay. And because our conscious awareness lags slightly behind (up to 7 seconds) what happens, our subconscious has already encoded what happened, including its consequences, and compels us to respond in a certain way—based on our past patterns and conditioning. (W.P Banks and E.A Isham, Psychological Science, 2009, 20:17-21)

The choices we think we've made consciously have already been made subconsciously. Our brain has fooled us into thinking our conscious choices are free will choices. (Fried, Mukamel and Kreiman, Neuron, 2011, 69:548-562).

Our PreEarthness and Earthness

When we browse the Internet, pictures and corresponding virtual data get downloaded in our neuroverse. When we browse our universe, images—thanx to astronomers—get downloaded in our neuroverse as well. There's a part of us—our Selfplex*—that's familiar with what's being downloaded, because it's a part of our personal preEarth and/or Earth history.

*See my Subconscious Selfplex Depot post.

Talking Heads

Some people talk to themselves. Others talk in their sleep. A good many talk to their golf clubs, cars, computers, pets, etc. When spiritual leaders talk too metaphysical, their audience sleeps.

A Sense of Belonging and Mattering

When we have a sense of belonging and mattering to those close to us, and to those in our orbit, there's an unflappability and confidence that surfaces which reinforces our self-worth, dignity, and desire to make this world a better place.

Neurobics

Researchers have coined the term 'neurobics' for tasks which activate the brain's own biochemical pathways and to bring new pathways online that can help to strengthen and preserve brain circuits. For example, brush your teeth with your 'other' hand, take a new route to work, or choose your clothes based on sense of touch rather than sight. Of course, we believe metaphysically interpreting religious scriptures is neurobic too.

We're Gobsmacked

We're gobsmacked* every time we get a compelling intuition, serendipitous aha, incredible divine guidance, and deeply moving insight later that day or a day after a meditation, which we believe connects us with the Field of Infinite Potential.

> *Gobsmacked is an informal British expression that means being overwhelmed with wonder, astounded, surprised, or shocked.

Symbiotic Belongings

Your thoughts, !ncl!nat!ons, intentions, emotions, choices, and actions are your symbiotic belongings.

Somatic Apprenticeship

Know that your earth life is but one school of unfoldment. It's 'skin school.' It's a somatic apprenticeship. It's an inning not an ending. It's you fancying your soul growth. Be absolutely clear about this, your human body is a garment you wear to clothe your choice to become the physical being that you are. It's your biological address. It's the 'somatic spacetime suit' you've constructed to house your particular version of Spirit.

Treeology

It's better to hug a tree than to bark up the wrong tree.

Psychic Synchronicities

Our psi abilities that are ushered in, are the products of many synchronicities and contemporaneous occurrences that combine in some fashion to manifest a particular psi ability which becomes relevant to a temporal event in the material world. Essentially, these synchronicities are psi equipment!

Instincts and In Syncs

Mystical moments heighten your superior instincts— AND—they do something else wonderfully well for you. They make it crystal clear that when it comes to ensuring your conscious alignment with your Divine Nature, do what your 'in syncs' tell you.

Supercalifragilisticexpialidociously Ordering

Supercalifragilisticexpialidociously manifesting our Greater Good means the same thing as Divinely Ordering our Greater Good. It's our own extraordinarily wonderful innate ability to divinely order our wants, desires and needs in our skin school experiences.

Getting Unstuck

When you want to get unstuck, become more flexible, and smooth out the rough edges in life use positive affirmations, an optimistic spirit, and a little WD-40.

Dogma Daze

Dogma daze is here! It's been here ever since we humans have been here. It seems that blabbering about the efficacy of truant dogma exposes the bankruptcy of highly dogmatic people's nonchalance in accepting evidence-based truth. However, we can—if we really want to—turn dogma daze into deep dive dazzle when we explore the depths of universal truths.

Karmic Forgettery

What if the Biblical 'mark of Cain' was retrograde amnesia? The author of Genesis reminds us that the 'mark' was meant to protect Cain (Genesis 4:15). Greek mythology tells us that before we incarnate we're instructed by heavenly guides (ascended masters) to drink from the Lethe River, whose waters cause returning souls to forget their previous life.

Lethe (the daughter of Eris, which means 'strife') was one of the five rivers of the underworld of Hades. Also known as the *Ameles potamos* (river of unmindfulness), the Lethe flowed around the cave of Hypnos and through the Underworld, where all who drank from it experienced complete forgetfulness and/or oblivion. In Classical Greek, the word 'lethe' literally means 'oblivion,' 'the swoon of forgetfulness,' or 'subconscious concealment.' Zeus also is purported to have drunk from Lethe before he's reborn, causing him to forget his life. Souls who drank from it forget their past lives and become clean slates for the next life.

In the Gnostic text *Pistis Sophia,* we're reminded to drink the 'Water of Forgetfulness' before we embody ourselves in another incarnation so we aren't burdened with conscious memories of our karmic inheritance from previous incarnations. However, our past lives 'karmic scripts' are warehoused in the deep recesses of our current subconsciousness so the gravity of negative karma (karmic clutter) can be expiated by our current thoughts, choices, and actions, AND our composite positive karma can enhance our karmic resume as we move closer to full and complete Self-Realization.

200,000 Years of Human Consciousness Summarized*

Awareness of having left Pure Beingness. Awareness of human experience. More wakefulness. Attentiveness. Alertness. Intelligence. Self-arousal. Self-reflection and Self-reference. Mental and emotional representations. Self-recognition. Self-protection. Symbolic association. Active thinking. Intentionality. Learned behaviors. Linguistic understanding. Cognizance. Experiential archiving. Imagination and creativity. Anthropomorphic God notion. Internal witnessing. Comprehension. Introspection. Intuition. Personal identity. Remembering. Predicting. Imitation. Sense of transpersonal mind. Free will. Moral conscience. Inner speech. Languaging. Explicit memory. Analogy formation. Quantum Beingness. Endogenous feedback. Rational control. Mental time travel. Highly emergent creativity. Qualia (subjective conscious experience). Universal beingness. Metaphysical and esoteric thinking. Clairvoyance. Audiovoyance. Precognitive experiences. Telekinesis. Apportation. Bilocation. Divination. Psychometry. Remote viewing. Retrocognition. Scrying. Telepathy. Influenced will. Transvection. Sense of a Universal and Eternal Omnipresence. The Field of Infinite Potential awareness. The Unified Field quantum physicists talk about. Sense of parallel universes, the multiverse and other dimensions of being.

There you have it: a partial, but (and that's a big BUT) concise summary of 200,000 years of philosophical, psychological, theological, metaphysical, and scientific speculation on the nature of human consciousness. Everyone agrees that it exists, but so far no one knows what it is, where it is, or how it works.

*Loosely adapted from: (Neisser, J., "Neural correlates of consciousness considered," *Consciousness and Cognition*, 2011 Apr 12; Mashour, G.A., Orser, B., Avidan, M., "Intraoperative awareness: From neurobiology to clinical practice," *Anesthesiology*, 2011 Apr 1: 1218-33)

Our Microbiome

Recognize that some of your best bio BFFs are over 100 trillion 'good' germs that constitute what scientists call our microbiome. These microbes protect us from illness. However, our overuse of antibiotics and consumption of animal protein kill these microbes as well as the harmful ones. Almost 80% of the antibiotics sold are fed to livestock to beef them up so they can be slaughtered for higher profits. This causes drug-resistant bacteria to remain on meat and spread to us humans, resulting in antibiotic-resistant bacteria. Your well-being is based on a healthy body as well as a healthy mind.

A DOSE of Happiness

Dopamine, oxytocin, serotonin and endorphins are considered to be the brain's happiness chemicals. The first letters of each of those happiness chemicals, when combined, spell 'dose.' So, engineer a 'dose' of this happiness cocktail every chance you get. When you anticipate something good, dopamine is triggered. Oxytocin triggers empathy, trust, intimacy and sociability. Serotonin contributes to boosting your mood when you enjoy something and feel confident. Endorphins help you 'power through' challenges, pain and discomforts by looking for the silver lining.

Zero Zeroed in On

Our limited understanding of 'zero' must undergo a triage. Most people associate zero as meaning nothingness. However, it, like 98% of our DNA and 96% of our universe, is filled with a 'somethingness' that holds 'allness!' Zero is composed of both infinite macroness and infinite microness.

Stop Feeding Those Self-Negating Critters!

One of the most powerful actions you can take for your spiritual growth is to take conscious control of the 'critters' trying to overtake your mind. You know, critters like: fears, doubts, false beliefs and assumptions; negative thoughts and emotions—all the stuff that's debilitating and draining. They can overtake you as surely as those wildlife critters can take over your yard, basement, or attic! BUT, you have the power to control them. All you have to do is stop feeding those self-negating critters!

Where's Your Lap Go

Where's your lap go when you stand?

Spiritual Orthopedics

Walking the spiritual path on practical feet is a journey of spiritual orthopedics which fosters inner peace if we want to step confidently and lively toward Self-Realization. It doesn't matter if our steps are on bare feet or shoed feet, big feet or small feet, white feet or brown feet or red feet, tired feet or energetic feet. Each step is a tithe toward our becoming one with our Divine Nature. The spiritual orthopedics of any truth walk requires steadfast faith, supported by love, wisdom, and zeal, multiplied by understanding and strength, and a penchant for divinely ordering every experience we have from the consciousness of our oneness with the Ground of All Being.

Re-in-car-nation

From a very young age I believed in re-in-car-nation. My parents bought a new car every three years.

The Efficacy of Altered States of Consciousness

Altered states of consciousness (psience) have traditionally been quite misunderstood and understudied by mainstream science. Why? For one thing, these anomalous states are difficult to study. The instrumentation hasn't been developed yet. They're not as easy as studying normal waking consciousness. To study our normal waking consciousness, you have people, mostly students and/or mice (mice and humans share about 97.5% of their working DNA), are studied in the lab where they have to press some buttons. I'm being simplistic, but you get the point. However, because of the nature of so-called altered states of consciousness, the process of getting people into these anomalous states so you can study them would be much more challenging.

The Future

When I say the word 'future,' the first syllable's already tucked in the past.

Endorsing Ends

Ends 'may' justify the means as long as there's something that endorses the moral legitimacy of the ends.

Enlightenment

When it comes to wanting to become more enlightened, don't suffer from a pain in the ask! Ask for guidance. Seek direction. Inquire about spiritual teachings and paths to explore. Examine the efficacy of various spiritual practices. Question all unquestioned answers. Call upon your inner Guidance and Wisdom.

Ahimsa

Ahimsa is a Sanskrit term that means compassion, non-violence, doing no harm, and respect for all of life. It's inspired by the Hindu belief that all living things are divine at their core and to intentionally hurt another living being with injurious thoughts, words or actions is to hurt oneself. If you believe in the nonlocal interconnectedness espoused by quantum physicists, you'll probably subscribe to this Eastern belief.

Coat of Many Colors

What if the well-known story in Genesis about the coat of many colors that was given to young Joseph by his father, Jacob is a metaphor for the human aura! The aura is an electromagnetic field (Human Energy Field-HEF) that surrounds our body and every living organism and object in the Universe has an aura. It appears to be made of many different layers and colors. Its shape and colors have been detected by using advanced bioelectric technologies and our aura appears to be oval. Auric colors that have been detected are: red and deep red, orange and yellow-orange, yellow, green and dark green, blue and dark blue, indigo, silver and gold, pink and dark pink, and white.

Researchers from UCLA, Princeton Engineering Anomalies Research Laboratory, St. Petersburg University and Bielefield University have all stumbled upon evidence that we do, in fact, have auras. If you're interested, check out the field of bioelectrophotography; research by the Princeton Engineering Anomalies Research Lab (PEAR) one of the most prominent psi research technology labs; and research by the Global Consciousness Project.

Dogmatic Lamppost

The light of the dogmatic lamppost keeps many people in the dark.

The Health Benefits of Forgiveness

When someone does something to hurt you, you can hold on to anger, resentment and even thoughts of revenge — or embrace forgiveness and move forward. Moving forward generally means going from bitter to better. And it's a more healthy direction to take for many reasons.

A 2017 study by the Mayo Clinic found the following health benefits of forgiveness.

- Healthier relationships.
- Improved mental health.
- Less anxiety, stress and hostility.
- Lower blood pressure.
- Fewer symptoms of depression.
- A stronger immune system.
- Improved heart health.
- Improved self-esteem.

Forgiveness doesn't mean you condone the act, nor that you have to be the person's friend. It has nothing to do with whether the person even accepts your forgiveness. It simply means you have the courage to release the attachment you have to the hurtfulness so it doesn't form an outpost in your consciousness. As a spiritual practice, the *freedom* of a simple act of forgiveness can offset the *feedom* generated by the high costs of hatred, resentment and anger.

Resuscitative Timing

I've found it very interesting to have both heart-to-head resuscitative and head-to-heart resuscitative experiences.

The Multiplier Effect of Kind Words

In a study published in an online edition of the *Proceedings of the National Academy of Sciences*, researchers have provided evidence that cooperative behavior is contagious. When people receive kindness they tend to "pay kindness forward" by showing kindness to others. This cascade of kindness and generosity spreads creating a multiplier effect. Each act of kindness is like a "matching grant" of (reciprocal) kindness that is truly contagious.

The *multiplier effect* of kindness which sociologists assure us creates a sort of 'matching grant' of reciprocated kindness and generosity is acknowledged by Mother Teresa who reminded us that "*kind words can be short and easy to speak but their echoes are truly endless.*"

Kind words start with kind thoughts, of course, and kind thoughts spring from a spiritually-attuned consciousness, one centered in goodness, generosity, and love. The phrase may have been coined by Anne Herbert, who claims to have written "Practice random kindness and senseless acts of beauty" on a place mat at a Sausalito restaurant in 1982 or 1983.

Philosophy's Calling

Ph!losoph!cal thought will always be challenged and criticized - and that's terrific, because it means people are getting down to basics in terms of what ph!losophy itself stands for: challenging unquestioned answers!

The Chicxulub Impact

Around 65 million years ago an event is believed to have occurred that caused the extinction of the dinosaurs. It was called the Chicxulub Impact which was the result of an asteroid's or comet's bolide or superbolide impact (a missile-like fireball of a magnitude 14 to 17 or brighter) with the earth just off what is now the Yucatan peninsula of Mexico, more precisely 322 km west of Cancun.

The crater is more than 180 km in diameter making the Chicxulub Crater one of the largest confirmed impact structures on Earth. In March of 2010 analysis from the fields of climate modeling, geochemistry, geophysics, paleontology, and sedimentology from researchers all over the world concluded that the impact at Chicxulub caused the mass extinctions of dinosaurs between the Cretaceous and Tertiary periods.

A MetaSpiritual interpretation of this event takes it from external flesh and blood dinosaurs and 65 million year old terra cotta to internal conditions within our own current state of consciousness.

Soooo, let's interpret the Chicxulub Impact as if it occurs inside our heads. For example, suppose the dinosaurs represent old, false assumptions that have developed into monumental belief systems, which have slowed our spiritual progress. They're beliefs that have been around for many generations (changes in perspective) in our thought universe (consciousness). Also, suppose the asteroid stands for an extremely powerful spiritual insight or idea, which strikes our conscious awareness, transforming our existing beliefs so that all of our previous "prehistoric" assumptions wither in the face of Truth.

Interestingly, Chicxulub is a Mayan word that roughly translates as "tail of the devil." MetaSpiritually then, we could say devil refers to thoughts that deny our innate divinity. So, the impact of a powerful spiritual truth on a consciousness that denies our innate divinity can totally transform long-standing false assumptions and error beliefs into their higher spiritual essences.

Contradictory Nirvana

I love the chemicalization that comes with new evidence-based information. It gives me the awesome wherewithal to contradict my previous thinking.

Our Inner Child

Carl Jung reminds us that we have a 'Divine Child Archetype' within us. Emmet Fox referred to it as a 'Wonder Child.' We call it our Inner Child, which is a psychic part of us, whose presence has been part of us since our birthing into the many dimensions of our incarnational beingness. Our Inner Child is timeless and ever-present, and not just a figment of our past. It's an ethereal, which you'll be pleased to know (perhaps even relieved to know) that isn't a physical child inside—unless you happen to be pregnant!

Our Universe

Sometimes it appears that the two most common elements in our universe are hydrogen and idiocy.

Quantum Ocean

Our world and all of the other interstellar worlds and suns are 'floating' on an invisible quantum ocean which is more, much more, mind-like than matter-like.

'From the Bottom of Our Hearts'

This phrase first appeared in English in the 1500s CE. However, the expression has been traced to Virgil's epic poem *Aeneid*, which was written between 29 and 19 BCE. The saying means:
- ♥ with intense feelings
- ♥ with sincere and deep feeling
- ♥ showing sincerity towards something
- ♥ expressing truthfulness
- ♥ saying something genuinely and honestly
- ♥ with utmost devotion

I'm going to start with the physical 'heart of the matter.' Physiologically, our heart has 40,000 to 60,000 neurons. In a normal person, the heart beats 60-70 times a minute, 100,000 times a day, 40 million times a year! During a single day, a ventricle pumps about 11,000 13,000 quarts [of blood], or 265+ million quarts in a lifetime.

Interestingly, the Chhandogya Upanishad speaks of what is known as the *hridaya guha*, or the cave of the spiritual heart (*kardia*), in which resides the Supreme Reality: "Go into the cave and you find the treasures of heaven." 'Heart' (*kardia*) means the center of anything. The core, the substance, the vitality, the very centrality of being of anything whatsoever is the heart of that thing.

So, spiritual kardia embodies a deeper and more transcendental level of consciousness. It doesn't refer to the physical organ, but is always used figuratively in sacred writings to refer to the seat and center of human life itself. Our kardia is the center of every sentient being's personality, and it controls the intellect, emotions, and will.

Also, in the Chhandogya Upanishad '*Tat tvam asi*,' which means that the Omnipresent Universal Reality, Brahman, is what we are. So, the reason the heart is the deepest, bottom, most innermost part of us is that it reflects the Supreme Consciousness, our Divine Self. It's that part of us that has the deepest depth of feeling, the truest emotions, the most superior intuitiveness, that which is unfailingly trustworthy.

Soooo, from the 'bottom of our hearts' Cher and I celebrate your Divine Status, and wish—no, affirm—that the coming year will bring you health, happiness, inner peace, and financial abundance!

Spiritual Singularity

I felt gobsmacked after one of my ph!losoph!cal !ncl!nat!ons. Just as living organisms spring from inorganic matter, gain sentience, and evolve into more complex thinking beings, we humans are evolving into even more Supersentient complexity and higher consciousness bandwidth which will help us achieve the Self-Realization we need to become consciously one with what I call the Spiritual Singularity. That means when we dump the concept of a primitive anthropomorphic god meme and realize that we're an individualized Life Force of the non-anthropomorphic Omnipresent Universal Reality (the Absolute, Überconsciousness,* the Global Omnipresent Divinity, the All) actualizing/ alchemicalizing as us in human form, we'll arrive at the Spiritual Singularity of All Beingness and Non-Beingness.

Okay. I realize a lot just happened here! I've moved your frame of reference to my frame of reference which takes you from a primitive anthropomorphic god meme to a non-anthropomorphic Omnipresent Universal Reality. The difference in perspective is huge! The difference in enlightenment is HUMONGOUS!

*Überconsciousness, Übermind is the Super-Conscious aspect of the Omnipresent Universal Reality. It comes from the German 'über which means 'considerably over, above' (rather than the taxi-hailing app, which is a lower usage of the term today). The etymology of 'über' means 'super-consciousness or meta-consciousness, something over and above ordinary consciousness.'

Two Sides of the Same Koan

It's become obvious to us that heads and tails, waves and particles, the manifest and unmanifest, light and darkness, giving and receiving, thinking and feeling, mind and matter, and our Human Nature and Divine Nature are 'two sides of the same Koan.'

Dialoguing With Realityness

Mystical moments are dialogues with the nature of Reality, not monologues. I believe the Omnipresent Universal Reality is real and we're still very, very far from understanding all of the fantastic anomalies associated with It, including us as one of Its most interesting carbon-based, human anomalies.

Our Universe

Our universe is both a ph!losoph!cal abyss and Eden, a mindboggling interstellar expression of the yin and yangness of Omnipresent Universal Reality's Isness.

A Reality Check

When you think about it, the concept of an Omnipresent Universal Reality is a collection of hunches—quantum physics hunches, cosmological hunches, ph!losoph!cal and neuroph!losoph!cal hunches, spiritual and metaphysical hunches, social science hunches, neuroscience hunches, epistemological hunches, religious hunches, Supersentience hunches, John and Jane Doe hunches, and Bil and Cher Holton's hunches, etc.

Technological Singularity or Spiritual Singularity

A growing number of people, including scientists, are concerned that one day artificial superintelligence will surpass human biological intelligence. However, I've got to say that my insperiences during mystical moments have shown me that there's more to the cosmic nature of our neurology than people think. There may very well be some sort of a technological singularity (artificial superintelligence surpassing certain aspects of human biological intelligence); however, I sense that our human biological intelligence will be able to significantly upregulate over time, *naturally,* to its cosmic level of intelligence through disciplined spiritual practices, what I call a Spiritual Singularity. After all, we are spiritual beings having a human experience.

Neuro-Yoga

In a sense mystical psi experiences, trance states, meditation, and déjà vu experiences are all forms of neuro-yoga.

Higher Ground

Just as one of the chief principles in warfare is to seize higher ground, the chief principle of gaining access to transcendental experiences is to up our normal waking consciousness to its Super-Conscious vibration.

Conversational Tail Bonking

In snowboarding terms, tail bonks occur when snowboarders intentionally hit and bounce off objects, either natural or manmade, with the tail of the snowboard. By analogy, a conversational 'tail bonk' is intentionally upsetting someone with a different perspective than you by inserting a controversial, maliciously judgmental and/or hurtful comment at the end of a conversation about the subject you were discussing as a seemingly spontaneous after thought.

We encourage you to refrain from tail bonking someone's choice to express certain beliefs and values. While there're differences in leadership beliefs, customs, and practices, etc., the intention of refraining from conversational tail bonking is to remind you to respect another person's right to express his/her management opinion. And it strongly emphasizes avoiding retailing disagreement for disagreement's sake, fear, hatred and purposeful discrimination.

Cher and I also encourage you to stay cool, calm and collected if you should ever receive a tail bonk from anyone intentionally bonking your beliefs. Your poise will speak volumes about your maturity and spiritual growth.

Human Apertures

We're the human apertures of our Divine Nature.

Paradoxical Doors

You're most likely aware that not all doors open in the same direction. Some are absolutely and unhesitatingly welcoming, others are obnoxiously a bit hesitant.

A Nirvanic Impulse

When you think about it, the intentionality of our desires is a nirvanic impulse, to be the beneficiary of a higher order of beingness that we know exists, but haven't felt yet in human form.

The Circumference Myth

What if there's no circumferential position from which to observe not only our universe, but the multiverse of which it's only a very small part of? Could it be that there's no inside vs. outside, no inner vs. outer, when it comes to describing the Omnipresent Universal Reality? If that's true, and it seems to be, then the notion of an interstellar circumference is a myth!

Detoxing Negativity

We invite you to recognize that worry, shame, guilt, anger, rejection, loneliness, low self-esteem and fear are the self-vetoing equipment in an unenlightened ego's emotional darkroom where negatives develop. These self-negating emotions are the materialistic ego's way of keeping you 'in line' in order to perpetuate its rulership over your human personality. They take up residence in an over-protective ego, one that's concerned about your welfare and survival, but (and sometimes it's a big BUT) over does its paranoia in challenging times like we're experiencing today.

Detoxing negative emotions will keep you walking confidently and poised on your skin school walk. There're hundreds of Rx's for negative emotions and the psychological wounds they cause. For example, you put bandages on cuts and take antibiotics for infections, right? No questions asked. In fact, questions would be asked if you didn't apply first aid or take prescriptions when you need them. The same thing holds true for your mental and emotional health? Here's the thing, mental and emotional wounds need 'bandaging' just as much as physical injuries do.

Some of the dazzling detoxes to add to your wellbeing resume are: concentrate on what you can do instead of what seems beyond your control; forgive yourself for putting yourself on a guilt trip, or for needlessly worrying, or for feeling shame; disrupt negative thoughts with positive affirmations; shrug off self-deprecating thoughts and emotions of all kinds; refuse to allow excessive guilt and/or fear to linger because these negative emotions are not the truth of who you are; ease any emotional upheaval by going 'into the silence' (deep introspection) where you know both the solutions are and the peace that passes all misunderstanding resides.

So, instead of allowing your emotional wounds to become open sores, open your wellbeing 'medicine cabinet' and use a combination of the following medicines: positive I Am statements and affirmations, visualizing healthy solutions, breathing techniques that center you and calm you, meditation, 'Dear Me' talks, nature walks, journaling, etc.

A Hylozoic* Wandering

What if spirit and matter are simply different actualizations (frequencies, vibrations, expressions) of the same Omnipresent Universal Reality (Eternal Essence, Allness, Infinite Isness)?

> *Hylozoism is the philosophical perspective that all matter is in some sense alive.

Your Point of Power

Every breath you take, every step you take, away from focusing on the 'now moment,' is a detour from your point of power.

Identity Theft

Our penchants toward unhealthy addictions such as drugs, alcohol, sugar, caffeine and gossip are all rooted in a much too prevalent chemical cosmology that takes us for a self-destructive ride. We believe they stem from an unawareness of, or the abject denial of, our innate divinity. Due to centuries of primitive anthropomorphic God programming we've suppressed and repressed our Higher Self and settled for imbibing self-imposed, counterproductive symbols of loneliness and identity theft - allowing our unenlightened ego to steal our attention away from who we really are—spiritual beings having a human experience.

What if we were 'addicted' to a healthy 'Self-Realization addiction': to health and wholeness, to loving kindness and compassion, to unconditional love, to forgiveness, to fair play, to smiles and laughter, to hugs and handshakes, to Namaste-ing everyone, to thanksliving, to

96

daily Sabbath experiences, to world peace, to altruism, to MetaSpiritual scriptural interpretation, to affirmative prayer and meditation, to spiritual practices (in general), to each other's welfare?

The Time-Out Room

Meditation is sending an unenlightened ego (mara in Buddhist theology) to the 'time-out' room.

Immortality's Mortalness

Life extension (immortality) needs to be accompanied by the kind of traditional and nontraditional medical wisdom and skill that'll keep everyone vigorous and healthy during their extended lifetimes. Don't you agree? Immortality's certainly a praiseworthy goal, one that stirs the imagination! However, when you think about its efficacy, it'll essentially require the simultaneous medical cure of virtually every age-related ailment that we know about and can develop.

For example, what good is curing heart ailments with stem cells, valve replacement, and by-passes, if it merely preserves more elderly bodies for ailments like Alzheimer's, cancer, arthritis, diabetes, atherosclerosis, benign prostatic hyperplasia, Parkinson's disease, etc. to steal? Also, there are other global issues to consider that'll affect our golden years unless we do something about them too, like pandemics, global warming, housing, food and nutrition, access to clean water, eradicating poverty, genetic modification, privacy, geopolitical minefields, dwindling natural resources, AI technological implications, etc.

Somatic Apprenticeship

Know that your earth life is but one school of unfoldment. It's 'skin school.' It's a somatic apprenticeship. It's an inning not an ending. It's you fancying your soul growth. Be absolutely clear about this, your human body is a garment you wear to clothe your choice to become the physical being that you are. It's your biological address. It's the 'somatic spacetime suit' you've constructed to house your particular version of Spirit.

Understand that your matriculation through different states of consciousness, in different dimensions of being, in rented vehicles (physical bodies), and in different spacetime continuums, is a journey you've chosen to make on your way toward the Self-Realization that comes from attaining full and complete Selfhood (your complete conscious One-ing with Omnipresent Universal Reality).

Futuring

The future starts the next consecutive-moment-of-now!

Spiritual Singularity

When humankind gets to the point in time when it dumps the primitive anthropomorphic god concept, and adopts the Pure Universal Mindlike Consciousness as the Omnipresent Universal Reality we will have reached the Spiritual Singularity that underwrites that epiphany.

'Wokking' Meditation

One of my favorite meditations is a 'wokking' meditation. You know—mindfulness eating.

Unicorn Mythology

The unicorn myth has very deep mystical roots. The interpretation we resonate the most with is its relationship to our pineal gland. The horn, emanating from the unicorn's forehead implies the existence of the mystical pineal Third Eye which replaced the boney unicorn horn. According to the ancient hidden wisdom traditions, the unicorn's spinal cord was presumed to extend beyond the *medulla oblongata*, and protrude through the pituitary gland and then out of the forehead between the eyes. This horn-to-inner-eye mythology implies that our exteriorly-focused physical senses, when developed to their highest spiritual essences, metamorphosize into their 'inner seeing' psychic counterparts. In this case, the pineal enhancement is believed to morph into a highly vibrational clairvoyance ability (clear-seeing extrasensory perception).

Going With the Flow

We're more ethereal wave than static particle, even in our physical form.

Überconsciousness

Our Super-Consciousness (Überconsciousness) is the Supreme Cognitive Summit of our Inner Life. And that's the place mystical moments take us.

Interrogatorily Speaking

Even as a child I became very much aware how questioning everything upsets people. And, as of this writing, I'm still amazed how questioning unquestioned answers tends to upset certain people. However, interrogatorily speaking, there always seems to be more questions than answers—doesn't it? Oh, that's a question, isn't it?

Our Biopharmacy

Our body, coupled with its mental and transmental powers and emotional wattage, is its own biopharmacy.

Upsetting the Applecart

Of what use is a ph!losopher* who doesn't upset anyone occasionally!

*Pythagoras preferred to call himself 'a lover of wisdom' or *philosopher* (a word he coined).

Interrogatory Legitimacy

Are all questions legitimate? Do all interrogatories have legitimacy? Should we ignore certain questions? For example: How many superpowers does Mother Goose have? Where does your lap go when you stand? Did the Hebrew Testament couple, Adam and Eve, have belly buttons? What color was the first horse? Why is the Earth the 3rd rock from the Sun? Why are unicorns silicone-based?

You can see from the above sampling of questions that even if a question is grammatically correct, it doesn't necessarily mean we have to give it serious attention. Or does it? The very nature of a question—any interrogatory— implies it will always get some kind of answer! Would it be correct to say that no question has ever gone unanswered? Wouldn't it also be accurate to say that some questions are answered before they're even asked?

The Immaculate Conception

When our intuitive intelligence, love, and receptivity to our Higher Supersentient Self are raised to their highest and purest spiritual essences we immaculately conceive a bona fide, inviolate Pure Idea.

The Third Eye is Eyed

By the way, a serendipitous bit of Third Eye research found Bil a few days after he posted this Cosmic 2x4 tidbit in his upcoming book, *My Mystical Moment Musings*, currently under publication. It's occurred to us after reading the research that even if people haven't been taught about the Third Eye, they know their True Nature and Divine Genealogy at a deeper level. Here's what science says in support of the Third Eye concept:

There's been some interesting research that relates to the Third Eye which I believe you'll appreciate. The researchers* asked the following question: "Where do you locate your true self?" The responses are verrrry interesting! Although the respondents' answers were slightly different where they felt 'I am located,' most referred to a single place inside their body—83% said the 'I that perceives the world' was located in their head, midway between their eyebrows! (That, as you know, is the Third Eye location)! This was true for people from all of the world's cultures, all age groups, sighted or blind, adults and children.

*Limanowski, J. and Hecht, H., Where do we stand on locating the self? *Psychology*, 2(4), 312-317, 2011. Mitson, L., Ono, H., and Barbeito, R., Three methods of measuring the location of the egocentre: Their reliability, comparative locations and intercorrelations, *Canadian Journal of Psychology*, 30, 1-8, 1976.

A Lapse of Riesling

Whenever I find myself less than philosophical, I attribute it to a momentary lapse of Riesling.

The Immaculate Reception

The Immaculate Reception is listening expectantly and clearly to the 'still small voice'—which isn't so still or small!

Wattage and Amperage

The wattage of our interior kundalini fire depends on the amperage of our spiritual practice.

Blushing

Did you know that we humans are the only species on our planet that blushes?

Unconditional Love

Unconditional love is the shortest distance between fundamental religions, New Thought schools, and Eastern faith traditions.

Cosmic Bliss With Landing Gears

We can be lost in cosmic bliss and still need to know how to find our passwords for our online bank accounts, Facebook, and Gmail accounts.

West Winging

Cher and I have been binging on the fantastic, whimsical, extremely well-written, and unbelievably relevant *West Wing* TV show. The characters are well-developed and likeable, the plotting is superb, the political antics mirror today's shenanigans, and the true spirit of America is captured.

Time Warp

The gravity of our descent (morphing, metamorphosizing, remodeling, shape-shifting) into matter hasn't only caused us to live in a time warp, but a consciousness warp as well. We've allowed the pull of sensory experience to keep us bound to this incarnational experience and consequently continue to increase the 'wait time' for our enlightenment.

The Speed of Light

The speed of Light may not be constant, although Einstein's theory of special relativity sets the speed of light at 186,282 miles per second (300 million meters per second) in a vacuum, many physicists today are exploring the possibility that this cosmic speed limit isn't constant, but changes, and changes a lot. Also, Light, at a certain vibratory level feels solid—and is called mass. Light at other vibratory levels is invisible—and is referred to as space! Our universe, it seems is composed of "now you see it, now you don't" Light quanta. Interesting, huh! Hope that sheds a little light on the subject.

Tomorrowness

When we're aroused by desires, we're in a 'before' consciousness — before we have what it is we desire. Desires take us beyond the now moment. They put us in the realm between nowness and tomorrowness.

Ph!losophy's Age Old Commitment

It seems to me that ph!losophy is committed to clarity, to carefully drawn comparisons and incredible distinctions, to uncover dogmatic pronouncements, to expose falsehoods, etc.

Ph!losoph!cal Playfulness

By their very nature ph!losoph!cal insights are open to many interpretations, because they're generally very insightful and sometimes unusual, yet playful, and are intended to be reinterpreted in the light of the expanding bandwidth of our higher sentient awareness.

Why Your Brain Needs Idle Time

According to neuroscience, we retain new information best when our minds are given time off to encode and consolidate. Even outside of intense study and memorization contexts, taking small breaks after digesting new material—whether it's a news article or an important email –appears to help our brain parse and memorize what we've just learned.

Our brain can get into its downtime state very quickly, and the education research suggests just a few minutes—five to 15—are enough to aid learning and turn new information into applied knowledge. Depriving our brain of free time stifles its ability to complete its subconscious integrative work.

Sooo, after reading today's Musings, enjoy a few minutes downtime before you rush into the rest of your day!

Transcendent Secrets

If you want more clarity and bandwidth of deeper understanding of Ultimate Truths, force your way into their transcendent secrets.

Psyched Out

Why is that you never hear about a psychic winning the lottery, horse races, or always picking the winning teams?

Cellular Theology

Each cell, every molecule, each of your atoms is a sacred tabernacle of the Omnipresent Universal Reality (the Absolute Isness, the All, the Global Omnipresent Divinity, etc.). There' no Interfaith posturing. Our cell's biology is their theology. When you realize the significance of this invisible connection you'll honor your human soul's relationship to your Higher Spiritual Self. When you acknowledge this connection, from soul to cell and from cell to soul, your body becomes the highly-charged sacred ground of your human beingness. When you achieve this perfect synchrony you'll experience the inner peace, joy, health, and wholeness which are the truth of who you are. So, cell-ebrate your cell power!

There's No Geography in Spirit

Since there's no geography in Spirit, it's all gee-ography!

Peace on Earth

The peace on 'earth' the mystics talk about is the inner peacefulness in our human consciousness (earth).

Déjà vu All Over Again

We rendezvous with ourselves hundreds—even thousands of times—in the reincarnational disguises we create on our way to our Self-Realization. However, if the truth be told, reincarnation isn't a necessary condition for enlightenment. Enlightenment doesn't have to be a long journey. When we consciously connect with our I Am Nature (a lower vibration of the One Reality that's the Ground of All Being) we become enlightened—and I believe we can morph into our enlightenment in one lifetime if we conscientiously and unapologetically seek our Self-Definition. In my opinion, the perfect déjà vu experience is *déjà vuing* with our Higher Spiritual Nature which is the 'True Us' before, during and after we become the 'Earthbound Us.'

Science, Psience and Spirituality

The evidence-based sciences and psiences aren't only compatible with spiritual perspectives, they help expand the bandwidth of those panoptic perspectives.

Extrabiblical Records

What if we find more extrabiblical documents, tablets, and ancient records during future archaeological digs in addition to what has already surfaced (the Dead Sea Scrolls, Rosetta Stone, Tel Dan Inscription - since I'm in this parenthesis, I'll add three more ancient records you may be interested in exploring: Ketef Hinnom Scrolls, Epic of Gilgamesh, Ugaritic Texts, etc.) that call into question the authenticity of what's previously surfaced? Would we be inclined to rewrite fabled history to clarify actual history? For example, what would the repositoried documents and archaeological finds in the Vatican Apostolic Archive tell us about religious history?

Toilsome Dogma Leashed

When scuzzy dogma enters the brain, it sees nothing but pet phrases.

The Voice of Reality

It's been my experience that you'll hear the 'Voice of Reality' the more closely aligned you are with your Soul Signature (your timeless, Distanceless Divine Nature).

Mirror Meditation

When we look at ourselves in the mirror we get an opportunity to see how our body looks: our facial complexion, our hair, our carefree smile, our posture and body shape, etc. The mirror becomes a visual tool for checking whether all those things meet our expectations and approval.

Using our mirror as a visual feedback system has other benefits besides a physical appearance assessment. If we add a little mindfulness to our mirror attentiveness we can turn our self-gaze into a lifechanging mirror meditation experience. It becomes a self-disclosure facetime experience that brings us face-to-face with ourselves.

When you look into your eyes, you are looking into your own soul. Make no mistake about it. You'll become aware of your own self-criticism and its visual effects on you. You'll see the 'mirrored image' whose the subject of your critique is you, its author! As you look at your reflection, you're seeing your own projection.

You'll become aware of your emotions and regulate them better. According to Daniel Goleman's emotional intelligence theory, the two main components of his theory are self-awareness and self-regulation of your own feelings. Once you become more emotionally-aware, the mirror teaches you to model and regulate your feelings. You discover that your attitude toward yourself translates into the one you hold toward others as well.

I hope this next statement mirrors my desire to show you how extraordinary you are! As you look at your reflection in the mirror repeat positive affirmations about yourself. Repeat them as often as it takes to see the image in the mirror consistently mirror the affirmations that confirm your extraordinariness.

Window Treatment

Sunlight bathes the whole sky from horizon to horizon. How much it can fill your 'house' depends on the nature of its windows.

Optimal Cognitive Investment

We all have an optimal daily cognitive allocation that represents our ability to do exceptional intellectual work and expand the bandwidth of our thinking. Every decision, big or small, every moment of mental focus, every time we choose something over something else, and every act of comprehension is part of our day's cognitive load.

The thing is, the conservation of our cognitive investments can be front-loaded by adopting habits for certain everyday mundane things while saving our higher cognitive functioning for higher order thinking.

For example, every morning, Steve Jobs would pick a black mock turtleneck from the top of a drawer filled with black mock turtlenecks. This act has a rumination load of zero. It's habitual and requires minimal decision making energy.

Most people chose what they'll wear each day from among 5-8 different options of clothing apparel and 2-3 different types of footwear, taking into account the weather, and who they may be spending time with that day. So, by the time they're dressed, their cognitive 'budget' has been depleted by 10-15 apparel decisions because none of their dressing routine is habitualized.

Everyday Steve Jobs would leave for work with 10-20 more decision dividends in his cognitive budget than most people do. People with his cognitive conservation mindset know that any habit you build into your busy day reduces your daily cognitive load, giving you a more expanded cognitive budget to spend elsewhere. Not every aspect of your life has to be filled with mundane options. Thinking this way lets you decide where your mental energy goes.

Don't Build Castles Out of Outhouse Material

Believe me, you don't want to build castles (higher spiritual perspectives) out of outhouse material (dogmatic religious malware that retails your loss of self—and the miniaturization, diminishment, and deprecation that characterizes fear, guilt and shame that's been retailed for thousands of years).

The Curvature of Dogmafication

Humankind must get off its carousel of indigestible dogma. The curvature of sleazy dogma is so circular that it simply makes you dizzy.

Fizzicks

Quantum physics needs to describe a universe that also includes *fizziks* (the ethereal psiverse).

Anti-Inflammatory 'Foods' For Thought

Certain foods encourage inflammation. An anti-inflammatory diet avoids these foods. Both saturated fat and omega-6 unsaturated fat are inflammatory, as well as: sugar and high-fructose corn syrup, artificial trans fats, French fries and fried fast foods, microwave popcorn, packaged cakes and cookies, soybean oil, white bread, processed foods in general, excessive alcohol consumption, processed meat (sausage, bacon, ham, smoked meat, beef jerky), to name a few health-busters.

On the other hand, Omega-3 fat is most associated with anti-inflammation. Monounsaturated fat, the kind that predominates in olive oil, are anti-inflammatory. Fruits, vegetables, whole grains, legumes, ginger, nuts, coconut water, green tea, tuna, salmon, and seeds, to name a few, are anti-inflammatory.

Also, personal behaviors like worrying, anger, resentment, stress, sleep deprivation, fear, and negativity as a steady diet are inflammatory 'foods.'

Our Timeless Neurobiological 'Churches'

Our mind, heart and brain interconnections are our neurobiological spiritual communities, churches, chapels, synagogues, cathedrals, mosques, abbeys, temples, parishes, tabernacles,

Dowful and Taoful

Touting the Dow is okay. However, following the Tao is better.

Your Totality of Beingness

Just as Alan Watts reminds us "The menu isn't the meal," and Alfred Korzybski chorused "the map isn't the territory," I suggest your human experience isn't your totality of beingness!

The Human Genome is Full of Viruses

Even after recovering from an infection there'll always be a piece of a virus encoded within our DNA. Approximately 8% of the human genome is made up of endogenous retroviruses (ERVs), which are viral gene sequences that have become a permanent part of the human lineage after they infected our ancient ancestors. However, endogenous retroviruses don't only harm our health, they can also be extremely useful for our survival.

It's been suggested that viruses are necessary for the existence of life in general. Interestingly, viruses have circadian rhythms like all living things. Virologists tell us we humans are basically just big piles of viral-like sequences that compose nearly half of our genome and seem to play an important role in our long-term evolution. In many ways, viruses are eerily reminiscent of the idea of ancient spells, which sit quietly as words in a book until someone utters the mystical syllables and unleashes the 'magic' contained therein.

Daily Deliverance

Give us this day our daily spiritual insights, and deliver us, dear Divine Nature, from all forms of malodorous dogma.

NASA's Amazing Space Telescope Will Peer 13.5 Billion Years Into the Past

The $9.6 billion James Webb Space Telescope is designed to capture traces of infrared light from the explosions that created our universe, that when analyzed, can tell scientists where light originally came from and how we got from the Big Bang to where we are today! It could tell us what Venus was like before it became a hothouse or what Mars was like before it dried out.

How to School Your Algorithms

Most of us interact with digital algorithms every day, whether we're exploring curated playlists, or looking for something new to watch. Video and music platforms like Netflix, YouTube, and Spotify each employ their own proprietary algorithms, designed specifically to sort out what we haven't shown an interest in and leave us our preferences.

And as algorithms' relevance grows in the world of media—and it will grow - so too does the complexity of their digital relationship with us users and their ability to create our very own personalized filter bubble.

We can 'school' algorithms by clicking on lots of content to 'teach' the algorithm, or moderate their behavior in other ways to curate an algorithm's (digital) eyes. We can engage in relaxed browsing, frenzied clicking, and even a certain nonchalance. We can make a wide range of deliberate and habitual content choices. We can click on diverse content just to observe how your suggestions change. You may even adjust your profile settings to see how factors other than consumed content impact the recommendations you get.

Black Cats

A religious creationist is a blindfolded person in a dark room looking for a black cat that's there, but hard to see, or isn't there at all. A spiritual ph!losopher is an open-minded person who finds it.

Forgetting Ourselves

We keep forgetting ourselves into another physical incarnation.

The Healing Effects of Meditation, Mindfulness, and Affirmative Prayer

Trauma often leaves us with distressed areas in the regions of the brain that control emotions, memory, and reasoning. These brain regions include the amygdala, the hippocampus, and the prefrontal cortex.

The amygdala is the area of the brain that controls our fight/flight/freeze responses. If it's repeatedly triggered by trauma, it becomes overactive. This hyperactivity leaves us habitually afraid, easily panicked, fearful, and anxious.

The hippocampus is responsible for warehousing our memories. The prefrontal cortex is responsible for higher cognitive and executive functions like problem-solving, memory, attention, and planning.

Trauma causes these regions of the brain to be smaller which restricts our memory, cognition, and emotional abilities. The benefits to our brain—and thus our lives - of mindfulness, prayer, and meditation are enormous. Not only do these three mental practices make us feel better by releasing helpful neurotransmitters, they can repair brain regions that have been affected by trauma.

Metapsychiatry is also a remedy. It's a spiritual teaching and healing methodology developed by psychiatrist Thomas Hora. Its aim is a reorientation from a preoccupation with material appearances toward the apprehension of spiritual reality. It maintains that the problems of humankind are based in ignorance, and may be overcome through 'knowledge of the truth of what really is.'

We're Bio BFFs

Our cells, atoms, and molecules are conscious beings. They know when we have their best interests in mind.

Your Unfailing Compass

For all the compasses in the world, there's only one true direction—the exact alignment with your Higher Spiritual Nature.

Virus-xiety

Anxiety thrives on uncertainty. And, as the coronavirus spreads, our unanswered questions can make us feel vulnerable and fearful. Here's what 'virus-xiety' does to us: the more we stress, the more vulnerable we can become to viruses, because stress can dampen our immune response.

So, take the basic steps you've been hearing about to protect yourself, your family, friends and others. Stay informed, but not overwhelmed, by the news. Proper hand-washing is your best defense against a virus. So, follow the evidence-based advice to wash for 20 seconds or more using soap and water. Or use hand sanitizers that contain at least 60% alcohol.

You may want to forego hugging and handshakes, embrace 'low-touch' salutations such as the now fashionable elbow bump, and protect yourself from contaminated surfaces (elevator buttons, doorknobs, door surfaces, shared work and public spaces, etc.) for as long as is reasonable and practical.

Also, spiritual practices such as meditation, mindfulness, positive affirmations, affirmative prayer and visualization are medicinal. They're the world's best antiperspirants in anxiety-producing situations!

We're Bio BFFs

Our cells, atoms, and molecules are conscious beings. They know when we have their best interests in mind.

How Many ...?

How many months are there in a mile? How many deep breaths are there in a smile? Is an indigo square, pyramidal or round? How many psychologists does it take to change a ...? Of all the questions we ask—our evidence-barren dogmatic questions are like that.

The 23 Psalm of Inner Peace

The 23rd Psalm is one of the most beautiful and often quoted poems in not only Biblical literature, but all literature. Although it's written in the language of a shepherd or herdsman, it can easily be updated adapted into the language of any human need.

I've placed it in the context of meeting unprecedented modern day human challenges. I offer it as a spiritual salve and affirmative prayer to help ease your concern and inspire you to trust the magnificent healing power of not only your Higher Spiritual Nature, but our mutual collective healing power when, together, we can achieve our Greater Good. Affirm prayerfully and expectantly:

Our collective Divine Essence is our healing power,

We can conquer any fear and eliminate any and all panic.

We're able to transcend all patterns of doubt, apprehension, and disquiet because our Human Nature is in sync with our extraordinary Divine Nature.

We can restore our sense of calmness and inner peace by having dominion over our thoughts, choices, words and actions.

We can do this by upping our consciousness to a Super-Conscious octave for the sake of being one with our timeless Divine Nature.

Yea, though we may be surrounded by the fear, confusion, and uncertainty of the coronavirus Covid-19, we will fear no pandemic evil.

Our Indwelling Divine Genealogy underwrites our well-being.

By right of consciousness, we anoint humankind with health, wellness and limitless vitality.

Surely radiant health and wholeness shall characterize our collective human experience;

And we will dwell in a consciousness of perfect health, respectfulness, compassion and oneness forever.

And so it is. And it shall be so!

Altered States of Consciousness Archaeology

When you think about it, past life regressions and lives-between-lives regressions are forms of altered states of consciousness archaeology. They help us dig deeply into our inner space realm so we can find neuro-artifacts (hidden treasures) of our incredible interdimensional Divine Nature. By the way, there's a branch of archaeology called intuitive archaeology you may want to check out.

Brainless Dumbing Downness

Many people think they're thinking clearly when they're simply rearranging their dogmas and confirmation biases.

Psyched Out

I haven't developed my psychic mediumship yet, or my well doneness as a psychic; however, I've experienced psychic rareness upon occasion, so I suspect my psychic abilities are generally dormant, or repressed, or just a gene uptick away.

Adamic Arsenic

The unenlightened, skin-encapsulated ego is a form of Adamic arsenic. It is poisonous (arsenic) to your spiritual growth. The instability you feel when you refuse to acknowledge your Divine Core is the plight of an unenlightened ego. In a very real sense, an unenlightened ego is the antithesis of spiritual growth. An anti-spiritual growth mentality sees separation, breeds separation, and leads to a life of unnecessary isolation from your Higher Spiritual Self and literally cultivates a propensity toward darkness and despair. What makes your recalcitrant ego especially paranoid at any level of your spiritual development is that it realizes it must be totally subordinated (become totally selfless and accepting) by being absorbed into your Deeper Self (Divine Nature or Higher Spiritual Self) if you're to become a fully illuminated being.

Speaking Truth

Always speak your own truth. Speaking someone's else's is unhygienic.

Badware

Bad habits and divinity-denying thoughts and actions are all forms of badware, and badware ultimately leads to soul decay. They're tough to unravel and criticism about them usually leads to ill feelings and defensiveness. If you've ever tried to untangle a piece of string, you know that yanking on it or pulling too hard only makes unraveling it more difficult. Sometimes you can untie it with your fingers. Other times you have to use a sharp object to pry between the folds of the knot to loosen it. Occasionally cutting the knot is the only thing that works. The point is, the more entangled something is, the more effort it takes to free it from itself.

Apertured For Immortality

Most of the human species settles for looking at life through a finite aperture, without realizing that we have an innate infinite aperture to grasp Omnipresent Universal Reality.

Professed Beliefs

One of the dangers of owning certain beliefs and professing particular values is that you have many opportunities to prove them by your actions. If you're un-true to your beliefs or fail to do what it takes to honor your beliefs, it's the same as not having that belief at all. You've heard the expression "faith without works is dead." The same thing applies to beliefs, no matter how lofty or noble they are. Beliefs without complementary choices and actions are only professed beliefs.

Blingology

"To bling or not to bling?" isn't really the question. The real question is: How much bling do you need before you don't feel the need for more bling?

Wordlessness

Cher and I decided long ago that we must teach spiritual truths at all times—and if necessary, use words.

Shell Shocked

A turtle's shell grows at the same rate as the rest of the turtle, so there is hardly a need of concern of the turtle getting over-qualified for its shell. When the shell begins to look as if it's coming apart, it's merely growing; discarding portions of the old with incoming segments of new. As we grow, we too need to discard the things that are no longer working for us at our new spiritual level of awareness! So, we invite you to perform regular mental check-ups to be sure your thoughts, beliefs, values and attitudes are congruent with the Truth Principles you practice! Anything out of alignment needs to go!

Conscious Satsang

Satsang is a Sanskrit word that means 'gathering together for the truth.' Conscious *satsang* refers to filling your consciousness with thoughts, intentions and !ncl!nat!ons of higher spiritual truths to show your devotion to your spiritual growth.

Lost in Thought

One of the reasons highly dogmatic people get lost in thought is because it's totally unfamiliar neuro-territory.

Dogs Smell Cancer and Diabetes

Studies have confirmed the ability of trained dogs (Labrador retrievers, Australian shepherds, German shepherds, poodles, dachshunds, Dobermans, collies and Portuguese water dogs) to detect skin cancer melanomas by just sniffing the skin lesions. Studies of dogs and cancer detection are based on the fact that cancerous cells release different metabolic waste products than healthy cells in the human body. The difference of smell is so significant that dogs are able to detect it even in the early stages of cancer. Also, some researchers have proven that dogs can detect prostate cancer by simply smelling patients' urine. Others can gauge the blood sugar levels in diabetics, warn allergic owners away from peanuts, or detect when people with narcolepsy are about to fall asleep. People with phenylketonuria (or PKU) tend to smell musty. A faulty or missing digestive enzyme makes people with trimethyla-minuria (or TMAU) smell fishy. Untreated diabetics can smell like nail-polish remover. The reason I'm including this research is to remind all of us that our interconnectedness with all living things can be fantastically medicinal and holistic if we embrace our inherent oneness.

Cher and I leap over dogma in a single bound!
What's your Superpower?

Humming Right Along

Hummingbirds fly very fast to stay still.*

* The fastest recorded rate is about 80 beats per second on an
Amethyst Wood-star Hummingbird. North American hummingbirds average around 53 beats per second in normal flight.

Science Fiction

Oftentimes religious dogma doesn't get any closer to
science than science fiction.

Quantum Crib

Spacetime is the 'quantum crib' our Omnipresent Universal
Realityness has created to facilitate our journey back home
again.

Entering the Stream

Stepping into a stream or river symbolically means
intentional and disciplined Self-Unification (Self-
Alignment), affording us the opportunity to enjoy being in
the 'flow' of life-affirming currents of higher spiritual
thought as we unite consciously with our Higher Spiritual
Self. In Buddhism, truth seekers (initiates) who enter the first
degree of initiation are called *sotapattis* or *sohans* which
mean 'one who has entered the stream.' In Hinduism these
initiates are called *parivrajakas* which means 'wanderers.'

Errorville

A stone in your shoe, a bug in your ear, a speck of dust in your eye, a splinter in your foot, a bout with stomach flu, and a quarrel with your family are nothing compared to your divinity-denying thoughts, words and actions.

Merely Ph!losoph!z!ng

The point of ph!losoph!z!ng is to start with something that appears so simple and straightforward that it's not worth exploring; however, you soon find out that its paradoxical, labyrinthine, and enigmatic nature leads you into the depths and existential bandwidth of enlightened thought.

Faith

As you move forward on your spiritual journey, recognize it's a process of growing and developing your Faith Quotient—'Faithing it till you make it' through practice: affirming the Truth of what you know, denying doubt any power, moving forward claiming the good that is yours by right of consciousness! And become more aware of your divine genealogy! Bless the inflow and outflow of everything in your life, knowing that goodness underwrites all physical manifestation.

Fallibilistic Knowledge

This perspective holds that absolute certainty about knowledge is impossible. It admits that because empirical knowledge is oftentimes revised by further study and observation, all knowledge, except that which is axiomatically true exists in a constant state of flux.

Library of Alexandria Resurrected

The ancient Library of Alexandria in Alexandria, Egypt, was one of the largest and most significant libraries in the ancient world. It was dedicated to the Muses, the nine goddesses of the arts. It flourished under the patronage of the Ptolemaic Dynasty and was the premiere center of scholarship in the 3rd century BCE until the Roman conquest of Egypt in 30 BCE. The library was destroyed four times—in 48 BCE by Julius Caesar, in 270 CE by Aurelian, in 391 CE by Coptic Pope Theophilus, and in 642 CE by Muslim general Amr ibn al'Aas who burned the library on the orders of Caliph Omar. We'd like to suggest that the worldwide Internet as a whole is a 'sorta kinda' modern day virtual Library of Alexandria, a digitized Akashic Records.

Doing Nothing

Has it ever occurred to you that simply doing nothing is better than doing nothing busily?

Certain Uncertainty

To live confidently without certainty, without being anesthetized by uncertainty, is a sign of being in the world, but not of the world.

The Molecular You

Inside of your body, in the microcosm of your inner being, are the subtle vibrations of a molecular world. You're composed of communes, colonies, cities and continents of trillions of cells in action. Your body is filled with cellular life. You're composed of hydrogen atoms and subatomic particles like quarks, leptons, and gluons that were present at the 'big bang' that birthed our universe. Quantum physicists tell us that we're literally stardust as physical beings. The stardust, by the way, is from stars that died over billions of years ago. Subatomic parts of you are 12.5 to 13 billion years old. Other parts of you are a billionth of a second old. At a molecular and cellular level you're a universe that's designed as a physical container that houses your particular level of consciousness and spirituality.

You'll see that to simply describe your network of cells as only biological containers comprised of a nucleus, membrane, receptors, tubes, fluid, and genetic markers is to miss the point of your biological footprint. You'll discover that your cells are highly intelligent beings with an innate divinity all their own. Written into the biography of your cells are the mysteries of life and consciousness, involution and evolution, time and space, the universe and the Multiverse! Your cells are literally tabernacles of Spirit.

Rebooting

We humans go through reincarnations to begin again (hit the proverbial reset button). What do computers go through—reboots!

Unnecessarily Necessary

Once it occurs to us how well we've done without certain material things, we realize how unnecessary they are—and probably were all along! We intuit we'd been using them not because we necessarily needed them, but because we merely wanted them.

It's Not Rocket Science #1

It's not rocket science to realize there's something better than constantly worrying about the economy. It's not rocket science to realize there's something better than going through life with a debilitating habit or addiction. It's not rocket science to know that there's something better than being bored and burdened by meaningless routines. It's not rocket science to realize that there's more to life than debt; barely making ends meet; and the fear and doubt and disappointment which goes with a crazy economy. And it's certainly not rocket science to realize that there's more to you than meets the eye.

Sleeping Your Way Into Enlightenment

We wish we could say that all it takes is a good mattress, the right pillow and a glass of wine to get a good night's sleep. But just like there's no short cut to enlightenment, there's no quick fix to get the sleep you need. Lifestyle changes are a must to reap the rewards of a deep, spiritually synergistic sleep.

Schlepped Self-Care

Schlepped Self-care means taking better care of our automobiles, stock portfolios, fishing rods, plasma TV's, iPads and iPhones, and bling than we take care of ourselves. It means neglecting the vocabulary of our body, mind, and soul while expecting to gain balance and peace of mind. It means failing to consciously and consistently align our human self with our Divine Nature.

See No Evil, Hear No Evil...

Seeing no evil, hearing no evil, and speaking no evil would be a terrific human species-specific achievement, don't you think! You notice I didn't end that statement with a question mark.

Greek ph!losopher Epicurus put it this way:
Is God willing to prevent evil, but not able?
Then he is not omnipotent.
Is he able, but not willing?
Then he is malevolent.
Is he both able and willing?
Then whence cometh evil?
Is he neither able nor willing?
Then why call him God?"

What do your instincts tell you? You may want to consult the posts in this book entitled: *See No Evil, Hear No Evil, Speak No Evil; Evil;* and *The Devil's in the Details.*

Disturbing the Peace

I've found that certain kinds of ph!losoph!zing disturb the peace.

Chasing Immutableness

When you're engaged in thoughtfully chasing mind-stretching Eternal Truths, it's important to let the voices in your head finish their sentences.

Sacred Places

The world offers us many famous spiritual spots: Jerusalem, Mecca, Delphi, Mount Arafat, the Black Hills, Lascaux, Bighorn Medicine Wheel, the Giant Serpent Mound, Stonehenge, Point Conception, Mount Sinai, the Ganges River, Machu Picchu, Niagara Falls, Victoria Falls, Mount Everest, Lourdes, Mount Olympus, the Great Pyramids, Mount Fuji, Mesa Verde, Canyon de Chelly, Ayers Rock, Enchanted Rock and Chaco Canyon, to name a few.

We need to honor these holy places as symbols of our spiritual growth. We certainly need to keep them protected to remind us of their spiritual significance, yet we must see them connected with the rest of civilization and nature. They must remain integral with life's routines.

Holy places are good reminders of our connectedness and oneness and contribute to our sense of heightened spiritual awareness, and even a profound transcendentalness that envelops us when our 33 physical senses are involved. Our senses work better. We feel part of a larger and profound universal wholeness. It's important for you to know that holy places existed long before religions found them. How do we know? Because holy places are universal expressions of our individual and collective divinity.

A Balanced Diet

For some people a balanced diet is a beer in one hand and a pizza in the other.

Ph!losod!p!ty

When you arrive at a series of serendipitous ph!losoph!cal insights you've experienced ph!losod!p!ty (philosodipity)!

Modifying Our Language

It appears we can learn something from humpback whales when it comes to languaging our experience. T. Lehmann and other researchers have found that humpback whales alter their songs every year between breeding seasons. One year all humpback whales sing the same song and the next year they sing a different one—and the changes aren't random. The songs are modified during the breeding season as their oceanic experiences change. Both whales and us humans, then, are constantly changing their communication system to accommodate the changes in their environments and life experiences. As a matter of fact whales and we humans are the only two species that are believed to change their language—although dolphins and some species of birds are now thought to modify their language too.

Heavy Interference

Don't allow hearing tricksterish dogma, in all of its forms, to interfere with your ability to question unquestioned answers.

Soullessness

Anyone who professes concern about the welfare of others but remains unconcerned about the poverty that damns them, the social inequalities that bury them, the economic conditions that strangle them, the built-in dangers they face, and the prejudices that disenfranchise them is speaking from a value-corrupted position. Forgive us if that sounds a bit harsh, but you no doubt know, or have heard of, soulless people like that.

Hitting the Nail

People who have Ph.D.'s in negativity are peerless at consistently hitting the nail squarely on their thumbs.

Absolively Positutely

I've got to tell you that it's absolively, positutely unwise—anytime, anywhere, and for anyone—to believe anything that has insufficient evidence without questioning it.

Spider Silk Surgery and Spirituality

Spider silk is very elastic (it can even be used for violin strings). It conducts heat as well as metals and, by weight, is tougher than silkworm silk and steel. Spidroin is the main structural protein in spider silk. One gram of the protein produces about 5.6 miles of artificial silk—enough to make hundreds of silk screws that can be used for bone fractures. Isn't that incredible! The threads make good stitching material because of their very high tear resistance, tensile strength, and particularly smooth surface. Researchers are looking into more applications of how the fiber in spider webs can be used to help connect new nerve fibers and veins in us humans. The spider fiber could change how surgeons treat wounds. The higher consciousness message is that we must see the medicinal value and symbiotic nature of the interconnectedness we have with all living things as one of our primary quantum fields of study. This kind of relationship with living organisms and biosystems is part of the spirituality of wholeness and oneness that unites us in consciousness with the universe.

Psychosomatic Spacesuit

Our current carbon-based, silicone-added embodiment on Earth is merely a psychosomatic garment (an otherworldly spacesuit, a reincarnational extravehicular karmic suit, a dogmatic straightjacket, etc.) to house our particular version of our Divine Nature.

Spiritual Cemetery

A consciousness composed of repressed (unexpressed, discarded, neglected, silenced) spiritual thoughts, insights, principles, and !ncl!nat!ons is a spiritual cemetery. You can identify it by the political, nationalistic, cultural and regional tombstones that mark the burial sites of its prejudiced viewpoints which have buried any hope of oneness, unity and collective welfare.

Beyond the Intellect

I apologize for being a little bit brusque, but some people are educated beyond their intelligence.

A Forelsket Reaction

Forelsket is a Norwegian term that refers to the euphoria we experience when we first fall in love. We believe a *Spiritual forelsket reaction* is the euphoria we feel when we first come across a compelling spiritual truth and see its implications for transforming our lives. It prompts us to remain a student of awe and wonder. It pulls us toward newness, uniqueness and novelty. It tempts us toward freshness and surprise. It's the elation, exhilaration, glee, and bliss we feel toward high-falutin' MetaSpiritual principles and teachings that'll keep us interested—and deepened—as truth seekers and practitioners.

Upskilling

Spiritual growth and unfoldment, from atom to sun, are based on the voltage of your soul's urge for enlightenment and wholeness. Your skin school experience has limitations, but not as many as you might think! Because you are a spiritual being having a human experience there are things—plenty of things—you can do to expand your awareness by upskilling your esoteric knowledge and experiential depth so you can enjoy being Home. Higher thought is a lifelong endeavor. It requires an open mind and a desire to comprehend deeper truths. Upskilling your spiritual perspective places you at the cutting edge of human thought. It moves you past the limitations associated with concrete operational thought and the relative realm to allegorical and metaphorical thinking and the Absolute realm.

Unquestionable

You'll live at a higher order of beingness when your desire to question unquestioned answers exceeds your desire to believe anything you hear without questioning it.

Unfindability

There's something mysteriously unknown in both the origins of mind and matter. Perhaps what we're looking for in both cases is alchemically unfindable! It seems that fleshing out origins of materiality, let alone consciousness and sentience, from immateriality is still the best kept secret.

Burning Bridges

If you choose to burn a religious bridge, or political bridge, or relationship bridge, or ph!losoph!cal bridge, or any kind of bridge, behind you . . .

make absolutely sure you've crossed it first.

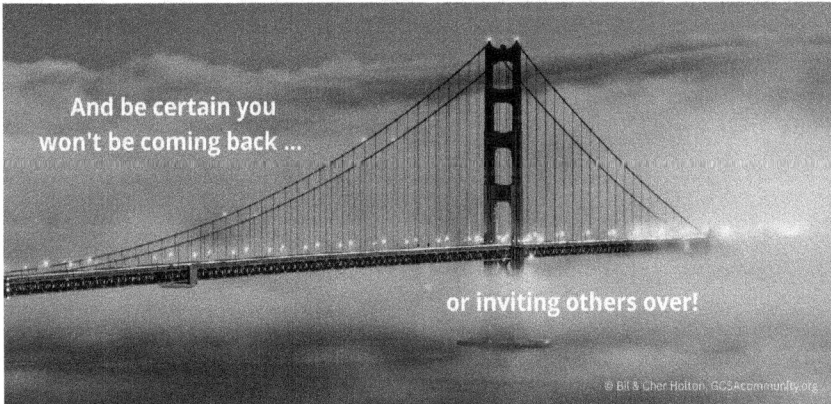

And be certain you won't be coming back ...

or inviting others over!

© Bil & Cher Holton, GCSAcommunity.org

Higher Consciousness Entanglement

Our species-specific higher consciousness entanglement, which is composed of the following traits—loving kindness, compassion, ethics and morality, fair play, and affirming a better world for all of us—is what has kept humankind from becoming extinct.

I use the quantum physics term 'entanglement' to describe the transpersonal interconnectedness of all living things that is manifested via psi capabilities which aren't just available for a select few, but for everyone (even animals and plants), because of various degrees of sentience leaning toward Supersentience. My vision of entanglement could very well describe the 'saving grace' nature of the best qualities of highly sentient beings.

Here's why—I believe the 'quantum entanglement' quantum physicists use to describe the physical phenomenon that occurs when a group of particles interact to share spatial proximity in such a way that the quantum state of each particle of the group can't be considered independently of the state of the others, including when the particles are separated by large distances—isn't the complete story, because capital 'C' Consciousness is a mind-boggling existential factor!

The fact that humankind is still here is a testimony to the apparent longevity of the better qualities of its higher consciousness entanglement. As spiritual beings in quantum form, we're eternally connected no matter what the physical, emotional, and mental distances are between us. With the current and future global challenges ahead of us, let's continue to strive to be in sync instead of extinct!

Hitchhiking

More often than not our left brain's decision-making capacity literally hitchhikes off of our right brains' superior intuition.

Evil

Evil is to live *sdrawkcab* (the word backwards, written backward! Live, spelled backward, is evil). Evil's also an acronym: EVIL = Ethics Violations Intentionally Launched. When you think about it, the 'axis of evil' is: Seeing evil and not stopping it; hearing about evil and not putting an end to it; and voicing concerns about evil and not doing anything about it.

The Virtual Assistant

Google has become our 'virtual assistant,' and possibly (no, most likely) yours too!

Busy Beavering Away

Busy beavering your way to build your life on over-indulged material possessions, egocentric power and status, and glutenous eating habits will damn-up your happiness, inner peace, and over-all health and well-being.

Karma

Do you know what the name of the oldest restaurant is in the universe? It's called Karma! There's no menu—you get what you deserve!

Commonsense Brakes

Confirmation biases, dogmafication, and Dunning-Kruger propensities are like a runaway bus without any built-in commonsense brakes.

Posthuman Nirvana

Posthuman nirvana could very well be where the soul and a silicone-based embodiment unite.

Dogmafying Fiction

A dogmatic dissertation isn't worth the paper it's written on.

A Reincarnation Hiatus

If you want to stop making the same mistakes over and over again, stop reincarnating!

A Misdialed Thought Conundrum

Just like dialing nine-tenths of someone's phone number correctly doesn't connect you to that person, not starting at the single, most enlightened preliminary thought won't get you to the understanding you'll need to 'up your consciousness' enough to grasp the nature of the origins of life.

Extending Our Humanness

Visualize what the evolution of humankind will look like as it integrates our humanness, transhumaness and posthumanness. Our humanness is an early stage of our sentient growth as a species. Can we make improvements in who we are and how we treat each other? Of course. As we become more transhuman, can you visualize how we'll improve our transhumaness? How will we—can we—should we - improve our possible posthumanness?

Will we commonsensically—and ethically—use 'NBIC' technologies (Nanotechnology, Biotechnology, Information Technology and Cognitive Science) to improve our evolving species? Give some thought to how the boundaries of our embodied reality have been compromised in the current age and how narrow definitions of humanness no longer apply.

Ask yourself—will our transhumaness and posthumanness foster our collective oneness or divide us as much as our mere humanness does? Journal your thoughts. Meditate on our collective acceptance of each other and on how we can co-create a future that works for everyone, including our planet.

The 13th Full Moon

The seminar speaker told us that the 13th full moon in a calendar year gives the serious moon watcher supernatural powers. Cher and I believe the speaker's a lunar-tic!

Spiritual Singularity

A Spiritual Singularity is the enlightened perspective of MetaSpiritual thinkers as they celebrate humankind's awakening to the non-anthropomorphic Omnipresent Universal reality that underwrites all that is, whatever was, and what will always be. People who are still stymied by their self-imposed, religious dogmatic whiplash will contribute to the lag time it takes to understand that Truth. However, I'm sooth-talking here, I predict that by the turn of the 22nd century, millions of humankind will be forward thinking enough to step boldly through the higher consciousness Spiritual Singularity Stargate.

Evolutionarily Speaking

It took evolution billions of years to hiccup, belch, and burp the sentient species called humankind. Perhaps it won't take us that long to smile, smirk, and grin our way to becoming a respectable Supersentient species!

Convergent Evolution

Convergent evolution occurs when different species develop similar adaptations or even appearances due to their shared environment, creating a similar, but not necessarily identical way of life. For example, dire wolves and gray wolves were the result of convergent evolution, and the stronger of the two (dire wolves) ended up becoming extinct because their food chain—which was different from the gray wolves—ran out.

By analogy, what do you think will happen when biologically-based humans and silicone-based transhumans share a common environment and yet create different ways of life that could result in one or the other becoming extinct?

Understanding the Whole

Ultimate Truths are generally described by the limited nomenclature used to describe them.

The Birth Canal Tunnel Phenomenon

When it comes to 'near skin school transition experiences' (NSSTEs), you've probably heard about people seeing light at the end of an ethereal tunnel which they've likened to the birth canal. Astronomer Carl Sagan had speculated that the sensation of moving through the tunnel was likely a memory of our passing through the physical birth canal during our birth process.

However, his theory was judged insufficient when Sue Blackmore, parapsychologist and meme-ologist, demonstrated via her research that people born by Caesarian section also experienced the birth canal tunnel phenomenon! Isn't that cooool! It appears that some speculations (sorry Carl) without corroborating research sound like 'tunnel vision!' Interestingly NSSTEs have reported seeing the future. Sooo, this seems like they're having life 'previews' as well as life 'reviews.'

Also, perhaps most interesting is the neurochemical origin of the 'tunnel' experience. Cells throughout the visual system are organized so many of the cells are in the center of the visual field and far fewer at the periphery. Sooo, when the cells fire randomly, the effect is like a bright light at the center fading toward the periphery. This neurochemical firing may very well be the origin of the NSSTE tunneling experience.

Norms Breached

Without deviations from stale norms, hidden treasures remain buried.

Beingness

The universality of Beingness transcends any universality of being.

Our Evolving Transhumanness

Is our universe wired in our behalf? Is the Multiverse? Is the Megaverse? Perhaps! If it is, it begs the question: In what form does that 'quantum wiring' take place? What if evolution (quantum wiring) simply involves the following eight spontaneous creation processes:

- simplification,
- complexification,
- diversity,

144

- specialization,
- mutualistic sharing,
- universality,
- sentience,
- adaptive natural selection!

Sounds sorta like a 'primordial soup' doesn't it—out of which evolves increasing complexity that leads to molecular self-replication, self-assembly, autocatalysis, and the emergence of multi-celled membranes, including us humans who probably aren't through evolving yet.

Sooo, that brings us to a follow-up question: Is our YOUniverse wired in our behalf? We say absolutely, because the YOUniverse we're talking about is our physical body (our neuroverse and bioverse). And the 'wiring' is due to existing transhuman* technologies like brain reading caps, gene therapy, cyborgization, nanobots in our blood stream, nanodevices throughout our body to guarantee our health, mind uploading, etc.

> * A transhuman is a person who is merely human, but has gone beyond the 'maximum attainable biological capacities' by incorporating cyborg engineering and silicon-based technological interventions via implants and AI-assisted augmentations that could very well transform most of our biomass into silicone-based physique.

Thoughts, Neurons and Neuroplasticity

Just as its true that 'thoughts and feelings held in mind produce similar thoughts and feelings after their kind'—it's also true that 'neurons that fire together, wire together,' which means that the more you use a particular set of neurons, the neurons than foster those processes neuroplasticize those connections and become even more neuroplastcized! When that happens a neuroverse that is filled with positivity, superior intuition, and clarity is more prone to expand the bandwidth of its Supersentient awareness, extrasensory 'downloads,' and intellectual capacity.

The Origin of Life

To our dismay (or perhaps relief) we humans still don't fathom where the origin of life came from.

Certain Success

Instead of waiting for 'the other shoe to fall,' expect a positive and timely 'shoo-in.'

Junk DNA

We came across some scientific research the other day that reminded us that we humans are composed of '98% junk DNA' according to geneticists. That means that only about 2% of human DNA actually codes for proteins. This 98% noncoding portion of our genome was declared useless genomic garbage until a few years ago.

So, it occurred to us that the importance of the interstellar connection between dark matter and energy (which make up 95% of the universe) and the 98% junk DNA which underwrites the other 2% of our genome that encodes for proteins could be the next two cutting edges in science and psience. What do you think?

Reincarnations are jukeboxes of
collective karma.

The Antahkarana Bridge

The *antahkarana* bridge (rainbow bridge, divine corridor, spinal column) describes the pathway of your entry into higher consciousness. This cosmic bridge (not to be confused with the beautifully written pet rainbow bridge) is built with the intent and mental substance of concentrated focus through many lifetimes. The quality of that focus becomes more refined as you achieve greater levels of Self-Realization.

Covidiots

We've learned that it's best not to associate with covidiots!

There's an Empowertarian in You

There's an empowertarian in you. Neuroscientists call it your 'Deeper Self.' It's the tenacious you, the confident you, the poised you, the resilient you - the extraordinary pandemic-thriver you! Viewing adversity as an opportunity and even as a catalyst to grow stronger is a sign of your inner strength and resolve. Mental toughness gives you the chutzpah to lean into adversity instead of back-stepping to try to keep your balance.

A DOSE of Happiness Hormones

Google 'mindfulness' and you'll get over 25 million hits. Giggle while you're being mindful and you'll send dopamine, oxytocin, serotonin and endorphins (a DOSE of happiness hormones) to 37.2 trillion cells in your body. Practicing mindfulness in the midst of bedlam and pandemics indicates the capacity to beam in selectively on things that center you while ignoring tidal waves of distractions that can capsize your happiness and inner peace.

Telepathics Anonymous

We were welcomed with open arms to a Telepathics Anonymous meeting last week. We didn't have to introduce ourselves.

Pandemic Moments

Anesthetize any negative thought, every self-denigrating !ncl!nat!on, and each self-defeating obstacle that surfaces in your conscious awareness when you're faced with upsetting pandemic moments.

Life-Affirming Relationships

When it comes to life-affirming relationships, personal and/or business, be a little more discriminating as to who is in your close circle of friends. Think about it this way— wouldn't you rather have four quarters than a hundred pennies?

The New You

Has it occurred to you that, where you are right now—this very moment—is the new you even if nothing major is going on in the world! The *you* that's reading this is a different you than the *you* before you read this entry. Each consecutive-moment-of-now there's a new you. Each now moment is a 'New Normal' for the you experiencing it! The new you isn't *defined* by old thought patterns. It's *refined* by your current awareness that they ARE old thought patterns.

Fine-Tune Frequent Friendscaping

In social media terms, friendscaping refers to the act of 'trimming' your friends' list down to a reasonable number so you can spend quality time with those left on the list which has become more manageable.

When it comes to mastering your skin school experience, friendscaping is the laser focus moment that means eliminating old habits and beliefs (friends outgrown) that used to define your old beliefs and perspectives in favor of new habits and beliefs (new friends) that are more in line with your current soul growth.

This laser focus practice invites you identify what you consider to be self-defeating habits, self-negating thoughts and behaviors, and self-limiting perspectives that conspire to derail you from walking the spiritual path on practical and prosperous feet. Make a list of these personal, professional and spiritual growth busters and prioritize which ones you want to friendscape from your human experience.

Lessen Self-Negating Learning

I don't believe we've chosen our Earth experience to learn specific lessons; however, since we're here we have many opportunities to lessen Self-negating learning.

Giving Permission

Joyfulness, faithfulness, positivity, optimism, and plenty of cheerfulness, etc., do not leave without being given permission.

The Right Time

The *right* time is the time we make *right*.

Being Aware of Schlepped Selfcare

Schlepped selfcare means taking better care of your automobiles, stock portfolios, fishing rods, plasma TV's, iPads and iPhones, and bling than you take care of yourself. It means neglecting the vocabulary of your body, mind, and soul while expecting to gain balance and peace of mind. It means failing to consciously and consistently working toward the authentic you, your deeper spiritual self.

I invite you to consider selfcare as soulcare, to value your soul growth as much as—and even more than—material things. As Cheryl Richardson writes in her book *The Art of Extreme Selfcare: Transform Your Life One Month At a Time,* "When we care for ourselves deeply and deliberately, we naturally begin to care for others—our families, our friends, and the world—in a healthier and more effective way." She further explains that through selfcare, "We become more conscious *and* conscientious people. We tell the truth. We make choices from a place of love and compassion instead of guilt and obligation."

Ask yourself these powerful questions:

- What one practice can I put into place this month that will improve my over-all potential?
- How can I be the best spiritual being I can be?
- What triggers will I use to remind myself to stay in sync with my Higher Spiritual Nature?

Our Universal Connection

We live in a thought-suggestive, choice-activated, action-centered universe.

Be Smart

If you're going to do something really dumb, and perhaps even ludicrous and baffling to those who know you know better, at least be smart about it!

Pay Attention to Material Discomgoogolation

Psychologists studying the high stress levels caused by Internet dependency have dubbed the phenomenon '*discomgoogolation.*' They characterize it as a 'feeling of distress or anxiety when unable to gain immediate information access.' Symptoms include forgetting to eat and sleep properly, needing more advanced technology to feed their 'fix,' more hours online, and experiencing genuine withdrawal symptoms when they are deprived of their computer.

We define 'material discomgoogolation' as the emotional state we find ourselves in when we realize we aren't allowing ourselves to move beyond certain material addictions. We believe similar symptoms occur when people who want to be more successful unexpectedly find themselves majoring in minor things.

We recommend what we call *sannyasinic* renunciation which means abstaining from overly-consumptive worldly appetites and materialistic cravings so you can grow spiritually. Sannyasa is a Hindu term for detachment from over-consumptive material wants by renouncing worldly thoughts and desires in order to spend our lives from a more non-material orientation. Downsize unnecessary bling and things. Eliminate any and all material addictions on you way toward mastering your skin school experience.

The Sabbath

While the Sabbath is a day of 'rest,' it's also a day of 'the rest!' You're able to do 'the rest' of the things you wanted to do during the week that work may have prevented you from doing.

Making Sense

Dogmatic proselytizers make noise with their mouth rather than make sense with their mind.

Tranquility Base

Perhaps the ultimate achievement of humankind will be the creation of a Tranquility Base, not Apollo 11's stunning Lunar Module landing on the moon on July 20, 1969, but within ourselves by completely aligning our Human Nature with our Divine Nature.

Recurring Coincidences

Coincidences piled on top of coincidences seems more like natural selection at work to me.

Reciprocal Value

My mystical and various other anomalous experiences have shown me that striving for a reciprocal balance between heart-to-head resuscitation and head-to-heart resuscitation is important for clarity. Otherwise, you'll experience constant skirmishes between head-centric pragmatics and heart-centered intuition when attempting to understand the nuances of Reality. Both head and heart need to get value points!

Geroscience Meets Archaeology

The more immortal humankind becomes as carbon-based beings (in addition to the longevity effects of our silicone-basedness), I suppose we'll become more interesting to both biomedical geroscientists and archaeologists.

Chaotic Ordering

Was our universe created out of chaos, or excited order? I'm asking the question; however, suppose chaos *is* excited order?

Evolution Takes Too Long

How can we humans who are used to mashed potatoes, instant oat meal and pudding, packaged cake mixes, frozen dinners, and smart phone Facetime believe it took billions of years for us to evolve as a species?

Pure Luck

Luck isn't as chancy as you might think.

Coincidentally Ph!losoph!cal

How many coincidences do you need to validate the truths associated with your spiritual and ph!losoph!cal perspectives?

Skin School

Hitting your thumb with a hammer, hearing bad news, bumping your crazy bone, sitting in the same position for an extended period of time, ending a long term relationship, getting Novocain to ease a tooth extraction or filling—are all numbing experiences. When you think about it our human incarnations are numbing experiences. We go numb because it's the soul's way of dealing with another skin school experience.

Our choice to enter into a skin school experience confines our awareness to a limited sense of self-identity due to our self-imposed confinement in choosing a human form. The somatic envelope (our physical body) we've rented comes with the karmic baggage of the human genealogy we've adopted and also a stepped-down consciousness that's consistent with the new life form we've chosen.

Our skin school experiences prune our conscious awareness of who we really are if our embodiments are the result of a restless and sense-addicted egocentric orientation. Essentially, we are prone to choose small-mindedness over open-minded universal awareness if we aren't careful. If we're not careful, we manufacture separation instead of oneness. As we become more awakened and illumined we remember that we're spiritual beings who've chosen a lower vibrational human experience and work toward re-aligning our human personalities with our Higher Self, our Supersentient Self.

The unfortunate outcome is that if you think skin school is all there is in terms of your total beingness, you'll experience the hazards of reincarnation after reincarnation until you realize your delusion.

Incl!nat!ons

What if an !ncl!nat!on toward ph!losophy is simply a lifelong penchant for discovering the secrets of Omnipresent Universal Reality?

Dogma Kennel

When strong confirmation biases, myside biases, selective fact retentions, cognitive dissonance, and a Dunning-Kruger perspective co-exist in one place it's called dogma.

Pancritical Rationality

As you no doubt have guessed by now, 'questioning unquestioned answers' is Cher's and my chief tenant when it comes to understanding reality. It's the process of decoupling fact from fiction. And it's also based on a little uncommon sense! It's similar to the pancritical rationalist concept which holds that every tenant of science and psience, or commonly held truths, should be questioned regardless of an authority figure's justification or assurance that it's true. Makes sense, doesn't it? Of, course, some people would rather live in fiction—and that's their prerogative. We've opted for evidence-based realism!

Divine Synchrodestiny

What if constant reaffirmations of experiencing the truths associated with your spiritual awakening that may seem like happenstance coincidences are forecasts of your evolving Divine Synchrodestiny*?

*Deepak Chopra coined 'synchrodestiny' which means taking advantage of unpredictable moments in our lives.

Roomies

Our interest in, and fascination with, quantum physics and its growing relationship with mysticism, spirituality and philosophy tells us that the dynamic foursome are fast becoming the most unlikely roommates. The conversation that begs to be addressed is if the quantumverse itself is sentient (and it certainly seems to be), then it must have some form of self-conscious awareness, just like us humans. Based on its behavior, the quantumverse acts as if it knows it's part of, and not separate from, a more comprehensive Omnipresent Universal Reality that actualizes as both wave and particle, and subject and observer, cruising at the speed of light and exhibiting pure instantaneous nonlocal beingness at the speed of Pure Consciousness.

Our Intuitive Compass

In the wisdom traditions, the Third Eye is the gateway to higher consciousness, and thus enlightenment. The Third Eye is often associated with clairvoyance, precognition, astral visions, out-of-body experiences, and astral travel. These inner 'knowings' are not clouded by egotistical thoughts, intentions or assumptions. They are instinctual messages that arise in you, seemingly from nowhere and often run in opposition to your rational thoughts. Soooo, follow your intuitive compass. Trust it. Its guidance is pure and its timing is exquisite.

Koan Nation

What's the sound of no thumbs texting?

At Our Core

After my meditation on August 18, 2020, which happened to be the 100th anniversary of the ratification of the 19th Amendment, I intuited the following thoughts:

If humankind were ever to develop a spirituality, philosophy, psience and science that could truly unify the human race and bring lasting peace, inclusivity, and equality to people and nations, it'll need to be based on the shared realization that all beings are, at their core, equal and have unlimited access to the knowledge of their own infinite beingness. It must be widely accepted that each of their hearts and minds is the individualization of the Omnipresent Universal Reality that underwrites our collective beingness.

In fact, I've got to say, that this recognition is the only understanding which can truly unite the world's people, and it must be shared by everyone equally, irrespective of race, creed, wealth, health, gender identity, spiritual and/or religious orientation, culture and nationality. It doesn't have to be earned because it's the foundation of everyone's essential cosmic nature, and everyone recognizes that primordial truth.

Writing

I've got to say, there are very, very few times in my life where I've found no pen or writing surface, no Microsoft word program, no desk, no set-aside time, no privacy, no inspiration, no natural !ncl!nat!on!

My Dutiful Privilege

As I look at my search to find Universal Truths, my dutiful privilege for humankind's collective soul growth is questioning unquestioned answers.

Uncommon Sense

Wouldn't it be delightful if common sense would more commonplace! Sometimes, I think you'll agree, there's too much nonsense that's pitched as common sense! As it turns out an ounce of uncommon sense is worth a pound of common sense.

A Holographic Microcosm of the Wholeness Macrocosm

Neuroscientific studies have shown that the moment we experience a sense of oneness during brain scan studies, there's a sudden drop of activity in our parietal lobe, the area in our grey matter that records the arbitrary distinction between 'self' and 'other.' Although researchers admit that the boundaries are blurred between 'self and other' they interpret their finding, from their scientific orthodoxiness, as a decreased sense of self. I totally disagree! I believe they've missed the point entirely!

It's been my experience every time during both meditational insperiences and mystical insperiences that the boundary between 'self and other' is completely dissolved! There's a sense of conscious Oneness, of discovering my unlimited cosmic essence, of realizing that I have a greater 'I-ness' which isn't separate from me. There's an enfolded

Wholeness-in-Motion of which I am - and you are - an eternally evolving actualization of the Omnipresent Universal Reality in human form. The physical me, it seems, is merely a Holographic Microcosm of the Eternal Wholeness Macrocosm.

The Nose Knows?

How often have you heard "It's as plain as the nose on your face!" The thing is, how much of 'the nose on your own face' can you see?

Dial It Up

The brain itself is dialed-up for intuitive flashes. Why? Because the synaptic connections that create intuitive highways in your neural networks are reconfigured grey matter that allows you to see things you didn't see before in a flash. So, dial-up your intuitive intelligence every chance you get.

Think

Never make anyone who's carrying a side arm uncontrollably angry! Never stand next to someone who's making someone who's carrying a side arm uncontrollably angry.

In My Mind's Browser

When things don't compute, we tell ourselves things like: "I need to reboot; In my mind's browser, I need to clear my cache; I need to navigate to a blank web page." As AI technology becomes even more algorithmic, it'll certainly be able to keep up with our carbon-based neuroverse. Don't you think? In many respects it already has! However, as of this writing, even EEG technology isn't sensitive enough to neural processes that register consciousness, which shows that neurophysiologists and psychologists still don't understand what to look for when it comes to fully understanding the neuronics of consciousness.

Ph!losoph!cal Inquiry

To be, or not to be! What kind of question is that?

Memeology

The most dangerous meme in any zoo, or anywhere else on planet Earth, is Anthropocene humankind.

Armageddon Postponed Indefinitely

What if no one shows up at Armageddon (that means everyone chooses to remain egocentric instead of subordinating their materialistic ego to their Divine Nature)?

162

Some Puzzle Pieces Are Puzzling

Jigsaw puzzles are Zen moments for me, and some of my ph!losoph!cal inquiries are meant to be puzzling!

Soft-Bodied Robots

I'm going to ask you to stretch your thinking as we wiggle our way through this musing by forming a soft-bodied robotic analogy into a spiritual perspective. Bear with me. I'll make it clear where we're going in just a moment. I'm going to base my admittedly loose connection on the intentionality of robotic design. For example, soft-bodied robots are designed to squeeze through small cracks, navigate through rough terrain and tight spaces, and are malleable and versatile enough to wiggle and worm their way into and out of any space or place.

Soooooo, I thought I'd draw an analogy between soft-bodied robotics and the malleability and versatility of affirmative prayer, meditation and positive affirmations. I've found these three powerful spiritual technologies excellent companions for helping us squeeze out of tough interdenominational tight spots, navigate around health challenges, smooth our way out of congregational conflicts, and finesse our way through important financial landscapes.

No matter how closed in we may feel in sticky situations or rough ministry terrain we can use affirmative prayer, meditation, and positive affirmations to squeeze through the 'cracks' in human personalities so that we can let our Inner Light shine. It doesn't matter how tightly wound a particular situation is, or how rigid the competing belief systems are, or how rough peacemaking efforts turn out to be, we can maneuver our way around error by using powerful affirmative prayers, meditations and affirmations to transform rigidity into openness and darkness into light.

Yin and Yang

What if coincidences are just co-incidences yin-yanging it?

Let There Be Light

In the traditional Christian scripture Genesis 1:3 says: And God said, "Let there be light," and there was light. We believe that means: Let there be awareness (light) that the One is many and the many are the One. That being said, we invite you to get out of bed with the embedded religious theology you've spent soooooo much of your time with, so the bed bugs (dogma, errant fallible scripture, the concept of a primitive anthropomorphic Judeo-Christian God meme, an exclusive mindset, etc.) won't bite.

YOUniversal Enlightenment

Here's my thought on fast-tracking enlightenment. There are no elevators or escalators to enlightenment. You'll need to use each of the rungs on Jacob's Ladder (the seven major chakras that run up your spinal column in your Vital Body) as psionic steps toward achieving YOUniversal enlightenment.

Social Distance Revisited

We've all heard a lot about 'social distancing'* when it comes to the pandemic. It's vitally important to do that, of course. However, we'd like to suggest another kind of 'So Shall I Distance.' It goes something like this:

Since we're all spiritual beings who've chosen this human experience, we have the power to affirm...
'So shall' I distance myself from fear.
'So shall' I distance myself from needless worrying.
'So shall' I distance myself from naysayers.

'So shall' I distance myself from not following health guidelines

'So shall' I distance myself from panicking.

'So shall' I distance myself from being intimidated by senseless biases.

*As Unity ministers, Cher and I prefer describing that health strategy as 'physical distancing' rather than 'social distancing,' because there's no geography in spirit.

Complement Sanitizing With Unitizing

During this pandemic challenge, complement your sanitizing with Unitizing! That is to say, apply timeless Unity spiritual principles like:

Thoughts held in mind produce similar thoughts after their kind. (So, think positive, life-affirming thoughts).

Work all things together for good. (Know that you can divinely order your Greater Good and affirm the Greater Good of others by right of consciousness).

Trust in the Field of Infinite Potential by manifesting what you want via Mind, Idea and Expression. (Recognize that you have the power to manifest from the unmanifest using those three universal 'calling forth' triggers).

The Opium of Dogmafication

Absurdity is the opium of dogma, and dogma is the ecstasy of closed minds.

Predestination Jitters

Just because we may be predisposed toward something doesn't mean we're particularly predestined toward that something.

Prebuttal Idiocy

The fundamentalist Christian Jesus' use of the Eucharist turns out to be partially based on the myth of Mithras' Eucharist ceremony. The two stories are sooo similar that religious fundamentalist's bafflegab claims that in an attempt to confuse the faithful, the Devil created the Mithras story to mimic the life of Jesus in advance of Jesus' birth!*

*Kingsland, W, *The Gnosis*, pg.99, Phanes Press, 1937; King, C.W., pg.123, *Gnostics and Their Remains*, David Nutt,1887

Manifestation Basics

On the Earth plane everything is dropboxed from the Ethereal Realm, created in the mind, recorded in the brain, downloaded via our choices, and manifested through our physical actions.

Morality

Morality is morale-building, don't you agree!

Demythologizing

We must demythologize the anthropomorphic God meme once and for all and follow science and psience, especially when science eventually takes us into the void, which is where the answers are.

Puppeteering Penchant

If we allow our subconscious patterns, conformation biases, poor habits, unquestioned beliefs, and ingrained dogmas to rule our life, we're puppeteering through life. These kinds of puppeteering penchants are aided and abetted by people who don't think very clearly.

Just a Rorschach Blot

When you think about it, the God meme of many world religions is just a Rorschach blot. Religious leaders and their famous disciples are telling us more about themselves and their own unenlightened interests and biases than about God or his son, the carpenter of Nazareth: Albert Schweitzer saw his God meme's son as a street corner prophet of doom; Oprah Winfrey says her God meme uses our failure to move us in another direction; Rick Warren says you can't out-give his Judeo-Christian God meme; Charles Spurgeon warns us that his God meme is exceedingly jealous; Joel Osteen assures us that his Judeo-Christian God meme wants us to be rich; Billy Graham tells us his Judeo-Christian God meme believes marriage should only be between a man and a woman; Joyce Meyer says her Judeo-Christian God meme is an invader; Pope Francis tells us that we're all children of his Judeo-Christian God meme.

The 'G.O.D.' of our understanding has none of those primitive anthropomorphic God meme characteristics. The 'G.O.D.' Presence Cher and I endorse is the Global Omnipresent Divinity—the non-anthropomorphic Omnipresent Universal Reality that is the Goodness, Wholeness and Interconnectedness which underwrite the Ground of All Beingness and Non-Beingness.

Eliminate Emotional, Mental and Physical Distancing

Eliminate the emotional, mental and physical distancing between the Human You and the Divine You—affirm your Omnipresent Oneness!

'Union' With the Absolute

'Union' with the Absolute doesn't mean obliterating the boundaries of individuality or negating your enlightened ego. It's simply evidence of your expanded awareness that you're an individualized Life Force of the Absolute actualizing as you in one of the zillion-billions of physical dimensions you choose to inhabit while you're actualizing your eternality.

Cyberpunks

What if intelligent machines become cyberpunks or cyberbullies—or even cybergods as they apprentice, and then overcome, our human foibles?

Don't Burst Your Ministry Growth Bubble

Don't be misled by 'bubblecovery* moments.' Simply stick to guest-to-member fundamentals for true ministry growth instead of spurious campaigns to simply attract 'butts in the seats.' Trying to fill your Sunday morning sanctuary with people who haven't grown beyond their religious dogma and aren't willing to grow spiritually, will cause your 'growth at all costs bubble to burst.'

*Bubblecovery is a financial term that describes economic recovery spurred by cheap credit which has a tendency to flow into temporary growth-generating speculative endeavors.

A Set Menu Approach vs Buffet Perspective

With more and more people becoming more spiritual than religious, we're witnessing a huge shift from a 'set menu approach' (dogmatic religion) to a 'buffet perspective' (open-minded spirituality) when it comes to the search for Universal Truths. For example, from our personal experience, we've found that dogma, in general—and religious dogma, in particular—are illiberal points of view, and they make open-discussions uncomfortable, let alone risky! Words are taken out of context by those who champion myopic dogmatic views and any open sharing tends to be seen as a green light to criticize, and even punish those with more open-minded, panoptically inclined perspectives. Soooo, how have we decided to handle truth verses fiction when it comes to soul growth? After a brief nano-second moment of soul-searching, we chose open-mindedness and questioning unquestioned answers over self-censorship!

Be Careful 'No-ing' Yourself

You'll find that Self-Realization is obligatory, and will continue to be obligatory in whatever dimension of beingness you find yourself while you're actualizing your Supersentience. Your Self-Realization comes from *knowing* your Distanceless Divine Nature—not *'no-ing'* your Divine Nature.

A Good Laugh

Ram Das once said, "If you think you're enlightened, go spend a week with your relatives." I got a good belly laugh when I read it. You may have just laughed good-naturedly yourself. I don't think his wisdom needs editorializing. Do you?

Our Evolving Consciousness

Finally, we spiritual beings in human clothing are giving the non-anthropomorphic Omnipresent Universal Reality something to work with—our evolving Supersentient consciousness.

Directionally Challenged

It's a well-documented fact that men are directionally challenged. They won't ask for directions. Why? Because it's in their DNA! This is why it takes tens-of-millions of sperm cells to locate a female egg, despite the fact that the sought for egg is, relative to its sperm suitors, the size of Nevada.

The Synth You

What if, one day, because of advanced AI technology, all that remains of you is the content of your brain wired up to a computer just before you die (you know, metamorphosize into your cosmic beingness)? That would certainly give you a digital choice for cryonic suspension, wouldn't it? And, what if the next version of you could be a Synth (a non-biological synthetic version of yourself) created by technologically enhanced, silicon-built AI scientists who want you to continue living as a technologically enhanced version of yourself. Or they could place your consciousness into another human body, which wouldn't necessarily look like you, or could even be the opposite sex of your previous physical embodiment.

You'd have your consciousness intact, but not your old physical envelop (body) anymore! If you decided to go the Synth route, your Synthness could be made to look exactly like you—a younger you, a more athletic you, a more intelligent you, an ageless you. How's that sound? And if you tire of each particular Synth-related rendition of what you consider to be yourself, you could simply select a new embodiment that captures your fancy. Of course, the question that begs to be asked is: How much of the new you would still be *you*?

Spiritual Obstetrics

Realize that the phrase "born again" is referring, in a very real sense, to a kind of *spiritual obstetrics* where we birth ourselves into a higher spiritual understanding which clarifies who and what we really are as Spiritual Beings in human 'clothing.'

Our Conscious Totality

Our conscious totality is no more within our physical body than Rachmaninoff is inside our iPhone or Alexa Echo.

An Expanded Me-Ness

I've thought many times, *I'm experiencing this fantastic Allness! An Allness that's an expanded Me-ness! A Me-ness that's greater than 'Me-now-ness!* Each insperience seems to have definite borders, yet I intuit that those boundaries are only products of my neuronic repertoire in my current human form. I've felt many times that there's an irreducibleness associated with each unitary now moment that's just a synaptic connection away from my being conscious of my own eternality.

Your Neurological Highway

As you place more of your attention on having a higher and more transcendental dialects (experiences), you'll move closer to your Higher Self and thoughtfully deeper into Its Supersentience. When you do that you'll experience more of the Universal You! And, as you continue to build (alchemicalize) your brain's higher frequencied circuitry, you'll lengthen and widen your 'neurological highway' and add more groves (lanes) to your grey matter, making your access to the YOUniversal You become easier and more fulfilling. You'll begin to seriously question unquestioned answers—and that'll be good. That'll be terrific! That'll be awesome! Separating fact from fiction will become one of your Superpowers!

You're Password Protected

You're password protected because you have immediate access to the greatest security system in the world: the Still Small Voice which is the Soundless Telepathic Voice of your Soul Signature. And the password is: *Peace be still.*

This Book

This book was written using 100% recycled letters and numbers.

Synchronicity's Pull

The gravitational pull towards synchronicity is one of the founding principles of the natural world. It's observable in our everyday lives and immortalized by quantum physics. Quantum physics teaches us that everything in our universe is made up of particles and waves which vibrate like strings at different frequencies. From the cells and subatomic particles in our bodies to the light and sound waves that echo throughout the cosmos there seems to be a resonance and synchronous connection.

Time Travelers

We're all time travelers in a cosmic stream of consciousness, altering our interdimensional sentient forms to grasp the nature of the Omnipresent Universal Reality (the Übermind, the All, Global Omnipresent Divinity, etc.).

Never Woo-Woo

It seems clear that we humans can only access a minuscule portion of the total 'experiential space' available to us in our universe. Not in a spiritual woo-woo way, but in a surprisingly rational way. We're endowed with 25-30+ meager physical senses and a mind that sometimes can't remember where we put our car keys, but we can begin to comprehend both the minusculeness of inner space and the vastness of outer space.

Religious Paradoxes

What if religious paradoxes are simply dogmatic scar tissue that hasn't healed.

The Basic Constituents of Reality

Contrary to the opinion of many people, capital 'C' Consciousness doesn't spring from the brain at all, but is instead a quality that underwrites all sentient matter and most likely all matter itself. That's not just me intuiting that. I've learned that there's a growing number of scientists, philosophers and metaphysicians who are beginning to believe the same thing.

That Consciousness (Pure Universal Consciousness) pervades our universe and fundamentally underwrites it is gaining traction for a handful of enlightened thinkers. This means that literally everything is believed to be conscious to some degree! And it suggests that even the basic constituents of capital 'R' Reality—electrons, leptons, quarks, omnipresence, etc.,—may very well have incredibly simple, and even complex, forms of conscious experience.

Updated Rigor

Rigorous, evidence-based, present-day scientific findings, at some point, will undoubtedly be over-turned and/or substantially modified—not by mindless anecdotes, or TV trickery, or imbecilic authority figures with financial and political backing, or evidence-barren dogmatic pontification—but by the current rigorous research at that time, that's based on new, updated scientific rigor.

A Coronavirus Group Healing Session

Cher and I proposed a group Coronavirus (2019-nCov infection) remote healing session today, Monday, Feb.10, 2021. It's a day after Sunday's full moon (called the Storm Moon), which is the perfect time to offer our group remote healing session for the virus. The 'storm' has passed is the healing analogy! We invited everyone who opened our email to visualize mass healing from 9 to 9:10pm to eradicate this pandemic. The idea was to combine our considerable healing energies to bath the entire planet with loving, compassionate, and highly medicinal currents of potent healing energy. People were wearing masks, of course, to help protect themselves from the virus—soooo, our intent was to also lift the 'mass confusion' associated with the disease and see the successful prevention and cure of this hurtful infection.

Enlightened Philosophizing

Enlightened philosophizing about our Divine Essence is really nostalgia. It's our desire to be Home.

Species-Specific Prana

Conscious alignment (Oneing) with our *Higher Spiritual Self* (our Higher Vibrational Nature) provides us with much more than spiritual attunement. The closer our conscious alignment (Oneing) is with our *True Spiritual Nature,* the closer our physical body's connection will be with the species-specific *prana* (Qi) that improves our capacity to resist illness and disease.

Paradoxes

People tend to trust their physical senses and to believe what their own experiences tell them, no matter how bizarre those experiences are. They'll layer explanations on top of their biases and perceptions about what they believe reality to be in order to explain away perceived contradictions and paradoxes. Since we generally experience the external world through dozens of our physical senses which are influenced (nudged, pinched) by our ingrained subconscious patterns and tendencies, we find it difficult to accept that these perceptions are sometimes entirely subjective and not necessarily reliable experiences of objective reality.

Let the Light In

Here's what we've learned about cognitive biases: Our cognitive biases (psychological blind spots) are our lenses to the world. So, we've got to scrub them off every once in a while, so light can get in. Each of us learn, after the first few years of our existence in skin school, to adopt the beliefs of those who preceded us as members of the human species. The human experience is new to us and adapting to our surroundings—weather-wise, culture-wise, and family-wise—makes the difference between how we see the world and how the world really is!

Soooo, for the first few years of our existence on planet Earth today, we tend to unquestioningly adopt the beliefs and biases of others—parents, relatives, friends, teachers, people in authority, etc.—to help us understand the world so we can maximize our human experience. We assume, quite naturally, that what we're told is true and accurate. And it's these early beliefs and biases that oftentimes become the foundation for building our own beliefs and biases. Soooo, we may have to scrub them off every once in a while, so light can get in.

Ph!losoph!cally Curious

If you're finding this book intellectually and emotionally stimulating, you are likely the kind of person who's ph!losoph!cally curious, open to new ideas, questioning unquestioned answers, and confident in your own thoughts. So, kudos to you. The world needs people like you.

Silicone-Based Sentience

Ph!losoph!cally speaking, once silicone-based AI is as complex as our human brain (with its carbon-based neurons), will it be as sentient and conscious as us?

It's Not Unknowable

We don't know enough about Omnipresent Universal Reality (the Überconsciousness, the All, etc.) to know It's Unknowable! And I suspect that, sense there's such a magnetic attraction for seeking Its hidden truths, that the hidden splendor within will be absolutely un-no-able!

Paradoxically Speaking

If wool shrinks when it's washed, why don't sheep, during the dog days of summer, get smaller when it's 100° outside and it's raining?

Exaggerated Hype

How many times have you heard motivational speakers say, "You can have it all!" when they're proselytizing success without limits? Well, they're selling you snake oil! You can have some of this most of the time, or most of that some of the time, or all of that some of the time, or none of this most of the time! Beware of exaggerated hype from exaggerators.

Keep the 'Art' in Artificial Intelligence

Remember when IBM's chess program Deep Blue beat chess champion Gary Kasparov in 1997? Well, hold on to your chess boards! On Dec. 7, 2017 another AI milestone was reached. Google's AlphaZero program defeated the Stockfish 8 program which was the world's computer chess champion in 2016. The Stockfish 8 program could calculate 70 million chess positions per second, compared to AlphaZero's 80 thousand chess positions per second. However, AlphaZero's success was literally guaranteed by its ability to apply the latest self-learning chess principles without ever playing a chess game! Out of 100 games the 'novice' AlphaZero program won 28 games against its expert rival Stockfish—AND tied 72. It didn't lose once! Guess how long it took AlphaZero to learn chess from scratch, prepare for the match against Stockfish 8, and on-the-fly develop exceptional creativity—4 hours! (That's not a typo).

As a matter of AI verses humans fact, at least in chess, creativity is already considered to be a trademark of computers rather than us humans. Perhaps AI will be another one of the self-administered 'tuition fees' we humans will have to pay for producing technologies before we have mastered the ethics and morals of their applications first! We, of course, believe we can. We also believe we must— by keeping the 'ART' (Altruistic Refinement Tendencies) in humankind's collective consciousness.

Perfecting Timing

You can spend time or invest in your timing and have the time of your life.

How Human Are We?

Biologists who specialize in researching our genome, microbiome and virome tell us that as much as half of all the biological material in our body isn't human! So, while our body is finite and just half us biologically, and our consciousness is infinite and most likely transcendent, with a modicum of subjective personal experiences included in our current mentalverse as merely part of us—how much of our spectrum of consciousness is really us?

The Universe Compressed

Our physical body is our universe's subatomic and atomic essences compressed into our size. And yet our entire universe isn't vast enough to encapsulate our YOUniverse.

Just Killing Time

Can you kill time without seriously injuring the eternality of everything?

Nonlocalityness

In the dark, entangled, nonlocal quantum omniverse, everything's happening all at once.

Our Emerging Transhumanness

I believe each of the 100 billion neurons interacting in our brain already has some level of sentient, and possibly Supersentient, experience. Perhaps we'll find they'll have some level of collective experience to perpetuate and sustain our personal identity no matter how transhuman we may become.

Time-Shifting

Time in the physical realm may be non-refundable, but in the ethereal, nonmaterial realm where effects can precede their causes, time seems to be refundable.

Moving Ahead or Falling Behind

On our soul journey toward Self-Realization it's as much as what direction we're *moving toward* as where we *are* on the path toward enlightenment.

Science Confirms It: It's Okay For Your Dog To Sleep With You In Bed

Research shows that 45% of people with dogs allow their pups to sleep in their beds. If more than 60 million US households have a dog at home, that's a lot of fur on the covers! Right! But there's no need to be embarrassed by this sleeping arrangement. In fact, research results show that both dogs and humans sleep together just fine, and the size of the dog isn't a factor when it comes to affecting sleep quality. Sooo, make room for your Mastiff or German Shepherd. There's room for both!

Not only is it common, but there are many scientific reasons to sleep with your pup. Here are just a few: Your pets help reduce your anxiety and stress levels, help lower your blood pressure, and provide warmth and security. Keeping your dog close can make you feel safer. If there's a sudden noise, your dog will alert you by a startling motion or barking. You can rely on your canine buddy to let you know if things are amiss in and outside your home. It's like installing a home security network without the quarterly bill.

Research also shows that if you have a well-behaved, happy pup, there's no reason why you shouldn't let the pooch sleep in your bed. In fact, sharing your space will most likely deepen the bond between you and your beloved pup. So, you see, it's a mutually beneficial scenario. Such a human/canine bond melts our hearts just thinking about it!

The Whooshing Sound

Have you ever heard the whooshing sound of a soul-deepening mystical moment?

Subjective Consciousness

I'm guessing that one of the qualities of the Omnipresent Universal Reality (the Übermind, Infinite Isness, etc.) is subjective consciousness or there wouldn't be subjective experience in physicality. And from my point of view, consciousness is a prerequisite of all experience, whether it comes from a robin feeding its young, a cat purring on our lap, a human enjoying a glass of wine, or a planet reacting to a meteorite strike.

Alphabiotic Thinking

We came across alphabiotic thinking in some of our research this week and thought you'd be interested in the concept. Alphabiotic thinking is stress-free, placebo-based thinking. From a spiritual standpoint it champions the conscious alignment between our body, mind and soul. It's the kind of thinking that gets us out of the amygdala (our fight, flight or freeze propensity which is reinforced by dogmatic religions) and into our neocortex (the seat of our higher brain functions which higher spiritual thought champions). Creating neocortex moments is what alphabiotic thinking is all about. It keeps us out of negativity and the myriad limitations championed by the amygdala, and moves us toward positivity and optimism.

Jeans and a T-Shirt.

We're lower vibrations of the non-anthropomorphic Omnipresent Universal Reality in jeans and a t-shirt, attached to our iPhones, driving SUVs, dreaming of nirvana.

We Aren't Strangers

When you think about it, we may have come back into this world via our mindlike consciousness, but our physical garment came out of it molecularly. Both the conscious us and the somatic architecture of our physical garment aren't strangers. Versions of them have been here before.

Dumping Dukkha

Dukkha is a Tibetan Buddhist term that means 'pain' or 'suffering' or unsatisfactoriness.' Dumping *dukkha* implies aligning ourselves with our Divine Nature so we can eliminate the unsatisfactoriness of some of our divinity-denying thoughts, choices, and skin school experiences.

Alchemical Nature

Our highly spiritualized alchemical nature that my *Book of Revelation, New Metaphysical Version,* talks about is a result of the blending of our superior intuition and intellect. Here's what happens: the feminine potencies (negative energy) are centered in the Heart Chakra, which is the seat of our superior intuition. Our masculine potencies (positive energy) are centered in our Brow and Crown chakras, which are the seats of the intellect. As we affirm the perfected body that will be the result of balancing both of these potent energies and nurture its readiness through proper exercise and diet, I believe we'll attain the glorified body alluded to in *The Book of Revelation, New Metaphysical Version.* And several of my unitary mystical moments have given me a glimpse of my ethereal nature.

Toe Stubbing

So far, to their dismay (or relief) neuroscientists, neurophilosophers, psychologists, enlightened spiritual leaders, parapsychologists, transpersonal psychologists, philosophers, etc., have stubbed their toes on the nature of consciousness.

A Minute Before

I'm interested in what happened during the first minute after the Big Bang that birthed our universe. However, I'm more interested in the nature of what happened during the minute BEFORE the Big Bang! And the minute before that! And the minute before …

Sword in the Stone

Exposing the truth by questioning unquestioned answers is a 'sword in the stone' test.

Take the Handcuffs Off Your Dreamscaping

There's a part of the anticipatory expectation process of dreamscaping (our term for vision boarding) that's been left out of (unfortunately) the guaranteed success formula as taught (inexcusably) by well-meaning New Thought vision boarding 'gurus.' And it's the vital part of the manifestation process that turns mere wishcraft into actually crafting your reality and making your dreams come true.

Neuroscience has the answer to the missing link in the dreamscaping process. The anticipatory expectation process is a frontal lobe activity that governs decision-making and goal achievement. When you expect a positive outcome, a rewarding outcome, your brain is motivated to work harder, *even when obstacles—no matter how difficult—limit or block your success!*

You can have a great looking vision board—plenty of stimulating pics and affirmations, images and symbols of success, etc.—however, only focusing on your desires can cause you to make poor decisions and create built-in limitations to your over-all success. Neuroscience provides a simple, but extremely effective solution: after you initially affirm and visualize your success, also visualize potential obstacles (salespeople call them objections), and then follow that up with visualizing solutions for overcoming them. This will make it possible for the decision centers in your frontal lobe to solve problems and widen your perspectives more efficiently and with greater ease.

What this means is you're integrating the instinctual motivational circuits in your lower and midbrain areas with your upper frontal lobe areas to maximize your over-all thinking and reasoning capabilities. In other words you're covering all of the contingency angles! This integration process is called 'mental contrasting' and is solution-focused to get the results you want. As Cher and I teach, it turns mere wishcraft into actually crafting your reality in less time than you might think.

Bottomline Selling

Religions sell fear, guilt and shame. As spiritually inclined Unity ministers, Cher and I sell YOUniversal prosperity, the Extraordinary You, and Self-Realization.

A Relentless Itch

We must outgrow the regimented and relentless itch of religious and scientific dogmatic bloating and transform those disastrous itches into the soothing itch for transformative spiritual and progressive scientific interests. We must become the higher consciousness trustees for helping to generate and accelerate our own species-specific enlightenment and Self-Realization.

Clairessence

To be consciously one with our Divine Nature is to have clairessence of our True Cosmic genealogy.

To Be Divine

We declare that to align our human self with our Divine Self is to be 'divine' in the sense of *divinus* (to gain extrasensory spiritual insights) in order to empower the highest and most elevated level of our human qualities and contributions to humankind.

Brain Hemispheric Synchronization

Use your left/right brain hemispheric synchronization as a fulcrum to leverage your spiritual growth and the quality of your innate extrasensory 'downloads.'

With the Greater Good in Mind

My ph!losoph!cal !ncl!nat!ons are geared toward discovering what's true and then using those truths for the Greater Good of humankind, our animal and plant cousins, Gaia, and our relationship with the cosmos.

Mental Portraiture

When you hear someone talk about the Omnipresent Universal Reality, or the Absolute, or Eternal Presence, what kind of mental portraiture appears in your mind?

YOUniversal Prosperity

I declare that each step I take insures health, happiness, inner peace, financial freedom, and debt-free living in skin school.

The Timeless Omnipresence of Capital 'C' Consciousness

In a ph!losoph!cally !ncl!nat!oned moment, I arrived at these insights: Our YOUniverse is Pure Consciousness as our total YOUniverse. A multiverse is Pure Consciousness as a multiverse. A megaverse is Pure Consciousness as a megaverse. The omniverse is Pure Consciousness as the omniverse. If these four 'verses' are manifest actualizations of Pure Consciousness, I wonder how many actualizations there are of Pure Consciousness in the unmanifest realms as well? By the way the unmanifest isn't empty or substanceless at all! It's filled with packets of light energy, sub-quarks, thoughts, fleeting electromagnetic waves, and virtual particles that pop in and out of existence at their own discretion, and, of course, the timeless omnipresence of capital 'C' Consciousness.

The Mother of Invention

Contrary to what most people have been taught (wrongly), necessity isn't the mother of invention. The mother of invention is focused intention, which is what leads to inventions.

Tricked by *Ad hoc* Magic

My penchant for ph!losoph!cally and constantly questioning unquestioned answers is refereed by common sense, open-mindedness, and evidence-based science and psience. A similar perspective is expressed by evolutionary biologist, Richard Dawkins: "I believe that an orderly universe, one indifferent to human preoccupations, in which everything has an explanation even if we still have a long way to go before we find it, is a more beautiful, more wonderful place than a universe tricked out with capricious, ad hoc magic ... by charlatans."

From Passwords to Passwordless

Is remembering passwords a hassle for you? Soon, you may be able to kick the password habit for good. Why? We could be moving into a passwordless world, which means certain applications for computers and other devices will be able to recognize us and protect our identity using something other than our old fashioned passwords. "Passwords are a 60-year-old solution built on a 5,000-year-old idea," says Jonah Stein, co-founder of the UNS Project (Universal Name System Project).

And it's going to be a good thing! Passwords are easily compromised using phishing scams, malware and data breach, etc. Turns out, the only real fans of passwords are hackers and identity thieves. Soooo, within five years it seems, we'll be using newer forms of multi-identification password clusters like: eye and facial recognition, fingerprints, security keys, fobs, our body movements, behaviors and habits.

Our brains aren't wired to squirrel away so many longer and more random passwords. And we're fed up with having to respond to 'password drift' commands like "Sorry, your password must contain numbers and letters, a capital letter, a hieroglyph, an emoji, an iphone icon, a foreign language letter …" We're exaggerating, of course, but you get the point.

Heavyweights like Apple, Google and Microsoft are already exploring high tech standards to verify identity. Perhaps it's just a matter of time when passwords go the way of the old eight tract tapes. However, it'll be interesting to see what happens to this "60-year-old solution built on a 5,000-year-old idea." After all, algorithms have been around since the 9th century—and they're far from being outdated. The earliest archeological evidence of religious ideas dates back 300,000 years or so, to the Middle and Lower periods. Perhaps religion will morph into spirituality or simply into a higher consciousness perspective one day without the need for 'denominational passwords!' You may want to pass that word around!

Coronavirus Concerns

If you're going to do any fasting over the Ash Wednesday-Easter events this year, *fast* from the fear of the COVID-19 outbreak. Instead, *feast* on affirming the common sense containment steps and perfect vaccine to eliminate the virus! Also, *feast* on lifting all of the people up in affirmative prayer who've tested positive for the virus and see their families and friends confidently and heart-centeredly handling any issues associated with quarantining and self-quarantining, seeking medical assistance, school closings, financial burdens, isolation, etc. Visualize positive and life-affirming outcomes here in the US and abroad.

Sometimes Less Is More

Consuming a half-pound of rich chocolate at one sitting stresses every cell in your body. Chugging a 32-ounce glass of beer is pruning your health and well-being. Pigging out on calories is ridiculing your body. Eating deep-fried foods and high-salt meals consistently is putting yourself on death row. When it comes to poor eating habits, less is more. All of these poor eating habits make it difficult to reach higher states of consciousness. They're not good for metabolism, and they're certainly not conducive for aligning your human nature with your Universal Überconsciousness Nature.

Enlightened Altruism

Those who are governed by enlightened altruism desire nothing for themselves which they don't desire for the rest of humankind—even during wars, downturns in the economy, and pandemics.

Beauty May Not Be Just In the Eye of the Beholder After All

When energy is poured into a system, and the system dissipates that energy in its slide toward entropy, it can become poised in orderly, indeed beautiful, configurations (spheres, spirals, starbursts, whirlpools, ripples, crystals, and even fractals). The fact that we find these configurations beautiful, incidentally, suggests that beauty may not be just in the eye of the beholder! Why? Are you ready for this? In the brain's aesthetic response may be a receptiveness to the counter-entropic patterns that can spring forth from Mother nature.

Kwashiorkoric Dogma

Gastrointestinalologists tell us that kwashiorkor is the protein deficiency which causes the swollen bellies of children during severe famines. Using that condition as an analogy, 'kwashiorkoric dogmatic bloating' is truth starved dogma and is the leading cause of a chronically undernourished belief system based on bloated religious biases composed of the absence of higher consciousness substance.

By the Winners

History is written not so much by the winners as by the affluent, the sliver of humanity with the leisure and education to write about it—from their biases.

Dwelling on Setbacks More Than Savoring Good Fortune

The psychological literature confirms that people dread losses more than they look forward to gains, that they dwell on setbacks more than they savor good fortune, and that they're more stung by criticism than they're heartened by praise. Psycholinguists add that the English language has far more words for negative emotions than for positive ones.

Boogie Woogie Appeal

Sin (forgetting our innate divinity) is the boogie woogie appeal of the senses.

Brushing Teeth

Don't brush your teeth immediately after meals which contain acidic foods and drinks (tomatoes, regular and diet sodas, citrus fruits and sports drinks). These foods and drinks can soften tooth enamel 'like wet sandstone.' Brushing your teeth immediately after meals can speed up acid's effect on your enamel and erode the layer underneath. Wait 30 to 60 minutes before brushing.

Lip Gloss

Vows are heart resolutions, not lip gloss.

Spiritual Rope a Dope

Spiritual rope a dope is protecting ourselves from the slings and arrows of life by using spiritual practices like meditation, affirmative prayer, visualization, gratitude journals, and dreamscapes so we can weather any storm, including pandemics. (In boxing circles, rope a dope means lying back on the ropes, shielding our face and stomach, and allowing opponents to throw punches until they tire themselves out so we can exploit their fatigue and defensive flaws).

Walking On Water

Metaphysically speaking, we 'walk on water' every time we rise above the negative emotions associated with our human experience.

10 Things You Can Do to Fortify Your Immune System During Virus and Flu Epidemics

In these turbulent 'Corona Times' there are ten things you can do to help boost your immune system.

- Get adequate sleep. When you are collecting ZZZs, your immune system regenerates.
- Take multivitamins. Vitamins A, C, D and E, vitamin B complex, and zinc are especially valuable for fighting infections.
- Keep a positive attitude. Make optimism work for you.
- Take hot showers that make you sweat. Why? Sweat contains antimicrobial peptides that are very effective against viruses. Also sweating helps detox your body against toxic substances, lowers blood pressure, and increases endorphins.
- Laugh your way to immunity. Laughter truly is one of the best medicines.
- Meditate. Meditation is medication! It has many emotional and health benefits.
- Eat foods high in fiber, zinc and antioxidants. Your digestive tract, your entire microbiome for that matter, destroys harmful bacteria. Eat plenty of citrus, fruit, broccoli, spinach, Tumeric, kiwi, sweet potatoes, and sunflower seeds and almonds. Zinc is immune friendly, so eat zinc-rich foods: eggs, whole grains, legumes, seeds, cashews, crab meat, lobster, chicken, swiss cheese, and oatmeal, to name a few. Steer clear of processed foods,

over-consumption of alcohol, and nicotine (they're all immunosupressives).

- Exercise. Exercise attacks bacterial and viral antigens.
- Clean your nose and wash your hands. When viruses take up residence in your nasal cavity they can cause infections. Use an alcohol-based hand sanitizer that's at least 60% alcohol for times when you don't have access to soap and water.
- Keep digital social ties active during physical distancing episodes. Pick up the phone, Facetime, Zoom, email, text friends and family regularly.

Dog-Headed People

Doggone it, there are myths about descendants of Cain, who inhabited Canaan before the Israelis and ended up populating the earth, that "barked like dogs and ate human flesh." Reports of dog-headed races can also be traced back to Greek antiquity. Augustine of Hippo mentioned dog-headed people in the City of God and thought they were descendants of Adam.

A Buddhist missionary, Hui-Sheng, describes an island of dog-headed men to the east of Fusang (a country east of Da-hanknown as the 'dog kingdom'). Marco Polo mentions Cynocephali indirectly while describing his travels to the island of Angamanian. Google 'cynocephaly (people with the heads of dogs).

Define Your Lifestyle

Define the lifestyle you want and then wrap your work around it.

Birthing AI

It's occurred to me to wonder if one of the unintended outcomes of the invention of Artificial Intelligence is simply to answer ph!losoph!cal questions about 'species' supremacy. Here's just one example, will us carbon-based human beings be smarter than silicone-based computers?

What If?

What if some historical achievements had worked out differently? Suppose Michelangelo - instead of, or in addition to—painting the Sistine Chapel Ceiling, had painted (or also painted) the Big Bang (which is believed to have created our universe) on the ceiling of a Renaissance Museum of Interstellar Space? What if Beethoven had written a Gradual Evolution Symphony, or Mozart had been inspired to pen the Intergalactic Multiverse Opus, or Rachmaninoff had felt led to write the Inner Space Neuroplasticity *Concerto*? Where might those classics have taken us musically, scientifically, and ph!losoph!cally by now?

Whirled Peace

Whirled peace isn't peace, it's chaos. And yet, chaos is excited order.

A National Geographic OOPs

A recent *National Geographic Science User's Guide* that's on the shelves today has several telling mistakes regarding the '100 things we never knew about our genes.' Two of these boo boos are the percent of our human DNA match with chimpanzees and the number of genes in the human genome.

National Geographic reported that there are 20,000 genes in the human genome. However, the human genome contains approximately 3 billion base pairs, which reside in the 23 pairs of chromosomes within the nucleus of all our cells. Each of the estimated 20,000 to 25,000 protein-coding genes in the human genome makes an average of three proteins.

When these differences are counted, there's more than a 1% difference in our DNA with chimpanzees. There's an additional 4 to 5% distinction between the DNA difference in human and chimpanzee genomes. There are 40–45 million bases present in humans that are missing from chimps and about the same number present in chimps that are absent from us humans. These extra DNA nucleotides are called "insertions" because they are thought to have been added to or lost from the original sequence. This puts the total number of DNA differences at about 125 million. However, since the insertions can be more than one nucleotide long, there are about 40 million total separate mutation events that separate the two species.

Our Zen Folks

I mentioned these two Zen masters in my book, *My Mystical Moment Musings*. They were our beloved beagle basset, Cleo, and our adopted toy puddle, Cinnamon, both of which we think were clairvoyant.

Chromosomal Comparisons

Humans generally have 46 chromosomes. In 2015 a biomedical article reported that a Chinese man had only 44 chromosomes. Also, some male humans (1 in 500-1,000) have what is called Klinefelter syndrome where the human male has an extra Y chromosome, making 47 chromosomes in all. A certain fern has over 1260 chromosomes; amoebas, over 800; hermit crabs, 254; algae, over 140; dogs and chickens, 78; cats, 38; horses, 64; giraffes, 62; fungi, over 60; alligators, mice, dolphins, 44; 40; 32; potatoes, 48; spiders and scorpions, from 8 to 84; platypus, 70. Antelope, water buffalo, and muntjacs (in antelope family), black rats, bentwing bats, zebras, lemurs, ground squirrels, beavers, all have 46 chromosomes.

Abracadabra-ing

In original Aramaic '*avra kadavra*' means 'it'll be created in (because of—my addition) my words.' So, divinely ordering our greater good is a higher consciousness form of abracadabra-ing what we desire from the Field of Infinite Potential.

Cuvée

There are two main uses for the word "cuvée" (pronounced KOO-vay) in the wine world. When in reference to Champagne, it refers specifically to the first-pressed (and most desired) juice. Outside of bubbly, cuvée refers to a particular blend of a wine, and typically of more than one grape variety.

It's a fancy-sounding word, so sometimes it's used to indicate a wine of superior quality or a special reserve, but the term is not regulated, so that's not always the case.

Brings a whole new meaning to Yeshua's turning water into wine story! Of course, MetaSpiritually, cuvée could refer to turning literally-interpreted scriptures into MetaSpiritually-interpreted scriptures.

The Census Misfire

I was gobsmacked when I came across this research: The author of Luke's gospel reports that Caesar Augustus ordered a census which required people to return to their ancestral home for registration (Luke 2:1-5). That meant that the Nazareth-based Holy Couple (Joseph and Mary) was required to travel to Bethlehem since Joseph 'was of the house of David,' which meant he had to go to Bethlehem to register.

Mary was pregnant with Yeshua (Jesus) at the time so she travelled with her husband to Bethlehem. While they were in Bethlehem the Christ Child was born. The census story is another one of the unquestioned answers (tribal dogmas) that Christians have believed without questioning its veracity for centuries.

The thing is, there's absolutely no record of any government authority ordering thousands of people to return to their ancestral homes to take part in a census. And the 'census idea' is especially suspicious since, as far as we know, marriage certificates, birth certificates and death certificates weren't issued 2,000 years ago!* Interesting, huh. Check it out yourself.

Also, the writer of Luke's Gospel reports that Caesar Augustus ordered the census when Quirinius was governor of Syria. However, according to historical records, Quirinius became governor of Syria around 7CE. If Yeshua (Jesus) was born when Herod was still king and shortly before the king's death (4BCE), as the Luke account mentioned above reports, Yeshua (Jesus) would have been 10 or 11 years old before Quirinius assumed his governorship.

It's entirely reasonable to assume that the motivation behind the author of Luke's Gospel to concoct the 'census myth' seems to be to make sure Yeshua (Jesus) was reported to have been born in Bethlehem to fulfill the Jewish messianic prophecy.

*The United Kingdom began recording births in church registers as early as the 1500s, but no compulsory, standardized system truly came to exist until the 1902 Act of Congress in the U.S., which established a permanent agency and standard registration system.

Spiritual Acupuncture

What if hugs, smiles, playful eye winks, compliments, kisses on the cheek, holding hands, rest, a soothing sip of hot coffee or tea, and mutual sharing of highly personal information are all forms of spiritual acupuncture!

Your Cellular Family

Here's why your cellular community can work health miracles: Your DNA is your master somatic blueprint and works as your bio-software... your proteins are your highly energetic evolutionary hardware... and your cells are your phenomenal pharmaceutical factories and paramedics.

Your cellular family is a living, evolving, adapting bioverse, which uses information to organize itself and to create ever-increasing levels of complexity. That makes your physical body more verb than noun. By that I mean your cellular architecture, sense of self, emotionality, and mental functioning have four-way conversations 24-7-365... supporting each other toward ensuring your—and their—continued health and wellness.

A-Musing

I love to live in the lateral, out-of-the-box thinking world, because there's a lot more room 'out there.' And that's the only place (state of consciousness) you're going to find the Muse who loves plenty of elbow room, too.

The Grand Designer Notion Revisited

To believe in a supernatural, deific, primitive anthropomorphic Grand Designer is drawing a curiously untenable conclusion, because it doesn't explain the origin of the supposed Grand Designer which turns out to be a nonfalsifiable concept! You can't prove it's true or untrue.

Quite frankly, the Grand Designer notion is taking the lazy way out. Where's the proof of such a Designer? Another way of putting it is—extraordinary claims require extraordinary proof! Not to belabor the point (well, I guess I am), to claim that this original Designer (an anthropomorphic God) was always there, having no beginning and no end, is illogical, wacky, goofy, nonsensical, and a bit flaky.

One more thing (I'm belaboring the point again), to find the origin (root cause) of the origin of life, you've got to find a legitimate path to uncover the root cause. Unfortunately, getting 'root-bound' in religious dogmas, some of which are moving ethics violations, allows no room for growth or for legitimizing a falsifiable path of least resistance to find the right answer, or any resemblance of the truth.

Subconscious Selfplex Depot

All of the world's great spiritual and religious teachers have one thing in common. It doesn't matter who they are, where they're from, or in what era they lived. It includes the gurus and spiritual masters, both men and women, who preceded Yeshua (Jesus), the Buddha, Krishna, Lao Tzu, Black Elk, the 14th Dali Lama, Mother Teresa, Thich Nhat Hanh—those who are living at the same time, and those who come after.

In every case, the one distinct thing they have in common is - they spent their entire ministry in the 'same place.' Sounds incredible doesn't it? But it's true. They've devoted all of their time and energy there. As do all great spiritual teachers. That place is a place called the *'Subconscious Selfplex Depot.'* It's our personal and collective subconsciousness—the place where all of our prepackaged, nested human and interdimensional influences, patterns of behavior, life scripts, faulty coping patterns, and egocentric defense mechanisms are warehoused. And it's a place spiritual teachers have been trying to get humankind out of for centuries.

Soul Spelunking

Soul Spelunking means having an interest in the dynamics and exploration of your various levels of consciousness (your subconscious, waking conscious, super-conscious, altered states of consciousness, dream states, past lives, multidimensional states of being, etc.). The exploration focuses on your small 's' self stuff (your Quantum Self incarnational material) in order to understand who and what you really are.

Where You Stand

You can stand firm, stand tall and stand anything as long as you can stand yourself. And, generally speaking, where you stand usually depends on what you usually fall for.

The Mindfulness Trinity

Awakened being, awakened doing and awakened having constitute the mindfulness trinity that will set you free from the centrifugal force of materialism.

Self-Conscious Choices

Most people keep themselves so busy and have gotten themselves so far behind that the future they wanted is gone before they get there. Some people, on the other hand, dream of noteworthy accomplishments, but fail to turn their dreams into reality. Too many people lose opportunities because they've lost themselves. And too many people have lost themselves because they are beside themselves with doubt, fear or pride. It doesn't have to be that way. Opportunities are one choice away.

Zagging Your Way Out

When your bad habits zig at you today, zag.

Centered Periphery

The closer you get to Self-Realization, becoming consciously one with your *Higher Spiritual Nature* which is the Omnipresent Universal Reality actualizing in human form as you), the clearer it becomes to you that the 'Still Point' at both Its center (your Soul Singularity or Sour Signature) and Its omniscient periphery (your Cosmic Divine Nature) are one.

Rx's for Professed Beliefs

If your professed beliefs aren't being translated into action, I invite you to give yourself a mental shampoo, followed up with conditioners like spiritual practices, meditation, positive affirmations, and questioning unquestioned answers.

Duct-Taping

Stop trying to duct-tape your spiritual growth by attaching it to unwholesome, toilsome religious dogma.

Spiritual Narcolepsy

Most people are sleepwalking their way through skin school totally unaware of their Divine Nature—that they are the human expressions of the U Omnipresent Universal Reality (Pure Universal Consciousness, the All, the Global Omnipresent Divinity, etc.) expressing Itself in quantum form as them.

Universal Cosmic Singularity

Cosmic Logos isn't an 'anointed' entity or a 'messianic' envoy sent to save humankind or any other 'kind' of being. It's the Pure Universal Consciousness expressing Itself as physicality. It's the world of subatomic and atomic particles, the world of forms, which are all quantum actualizations of the One Reality called Pure Universal Consciousness. There's no 'anointing'—or need for it—because that would imply that *something* 'anointed' *something else*! And that would imply separation when there is only a Universal Cosmic Singularity!

Changeology

All change isn't necessarily growth, just like all movement isn't necessarily forward, and activity isn't necessarily accomplishment.

First Things First

Breathe in and then breathe out. Inhale and now exhale. If you neglect to do this, any concerns about your enlightenment, or the best prayer technique to use, or the right church or synagogue to attend, or which password to use for your online banking will be the least of your problems.

Mindful Dancing

Cher and I began ballroom dancing as a spiritual practice in 1998 and discovered a new level of partnership and soulmateness that has enriched both our personal and professional lives. We competed nationally as an amateur couple in the American Smooth and Rhythm DanceSport Championships. Although we don't compete anymore we performed choreographed routines for showcases and exhibitions, and "invented" our own trademark routines for a time. Occasionally, we still dance socially for non-competitive fun. And like Friedrich Nietzsche's sentiments said so many years ago: *"Everyday (we) count wasted in which there has been no dancing."* For us, dancing is a moving mindfulness meditation. Each element is a mindful step; every pattern is a spiritual path; every dance, in its totality, is a cosmic union with the energies of our combined Divine Natures.

Errorville

A stone in your shoe, a bug in your ear, a speck of dust in your eye, a splinter in your foot, a bout with stomach flu, and a quarrel with your family are nothing compared to your divinity-denying thoughts, words and actions.

It's Not Rocket Science #2

The secret to mastering the art of living is not rocket science. It's aligning your waking consciousness with the *Extraordinary You* (your *Higher Spiritual Self*) before you do anything else, and you'll have the inner strength to do all you need to master the human experience. You'll be the beneficiary of: answers to financial concerns, career direction, inner peace, intuitive insights, the ability to challenge unquestioned answers, spectacular hunches, solutions to nagging family issues, phenomenal inspiration, deeper knowledge about truth principles, the ability to make wise decisions, and the strength to meet any skin school challenge.

Supersentient Awareness

Esoteric views (metaphysical views, metaphorical views, figurative views, analogical views) of Reality are views limited by your level of sentient awareness. Wouldn't you agree? There's no *"the view"* of reality because humankind hasn't progressed to the highest level of super-enlightened awareness (a Supersentient perspective). We're all unfolding in a sea of consciousness which is universal and unlimited.

Wobbling

You'll never grow in your spirituality if you try to move left and right, and backwards and forward at the same time.

Fairy Tales

The deceitful falsehoods, myths, misrepresentations, out-and-out lies, smoke and mirrors, ridiculous concoctions, delusions, fictitious monstrosities, unbelievable hallucinations, pretentious baloney, and whoppers the unenlightened ego tells in every waking moment are the fairy tales humankind has bought into for centuries.

A 'One Channel' Perspective

I've never been a fan of 'one channel' religion or one perspective guruship of any kind. A river can't flow with only one bank.

Mortal Coil

The length of our life is metaphorically a length of thread that is coiled on a spool, an analogy related to the ancient Greek mythological figures of the Fates. It was popularized by the "To be, or not to be," the "slings and arrows of outrageous fortune," and "to sleep, perchance to dream" soliloquies in Shakespeare's *Hamlet*. It was coined repeatedly to address the troubles, burdens, and possible opportunities life tosses at us.

At various times people have used it as a verb to mean 'to cull,' 'to thrash,' 'to lay in rings or spirals.' As we live, our 'mortality thread' is unwound from the coil by the shuttle of the loom of time and circumstance. So, the mortal coil refers to our tumults and troubles, our challenges and turmoils, the trials and tribulations, and the hard-won opportunities we face as spiritual beings having a human experience.

Self-Disclosure

I'm very much a fan of *Self-disclosure* (admitting that you are an individualized Life Force of the Omnipresent Universal Reality actualizing Itself in human form as you). Sooooo, *Self*-disclose! Affirm your divine origins! Celebrate your innate divinity.

Rheostated Wisdom

There's amazing power in radiating wisdom (*vidya*). Your inner wisdom is like the rheostat on a dining room light. As you turn the rheostat clockwise, you're able to regulate the light—make it brighter. Turn it counter-clockwise and it dims. And even when you turn it all the way down, the potential for lighting the room is still there! When it comes to your innate wisdom you can also turn your 'rheostat' up or down. Your wisdom is there waiting to be used.

Soul Intoxication

Soul (the human personality) intoxication means becoming inebriated (thoroughly engrossed) in the whirlpool (sense pleasures and materialistic appetites) of matter.

The Universal Universe

As far as we know the physical universe is the lowest, most dense, vibration of the One Universal Presence. And since there are many levels (facets, dimensions, frequencies, vibrations, etc.) of the Omnipresent Universal Reality (One Presence) in physicality the differences between these levels are more vibrational than spatial.

Nothingness

Nothing is interesting, when you're interested in nothing.

Youology

You're positively, absolutely the most qualified person on the planet to be yourself. You can be yourself any time you want. You can be beside yourself if you want, although Cher and I don't recommend doing that too often. You can be behind yourself or get ahead of yourself. However, one thing we know for sure about you—it becomes you to become the true authentic, moral, and ethical you every chance you get.

Unblurring

Unblurring is taking your materialistic blinders off so you can see the awesome spiritual landscape around you.

Eating the Menu

Too much theology and too little practice is trying to eat the menu instead of the meal.

Our Psi-Conduciveness

What if each of us has inherited naturally-selected, gene-prescribed phantastic supersensory intelligence (psi abilities) that are evolutionary adaptations specifically formed as survival mechanisms in addition to our daily extrasensory qualities which help us matriculate through skin school normality?

It seems reasonable that our psi qualities would evolve—can evolve, have evolved—in varying degrees of expression along with our other species-specific traits and abilities to help us survive and thrive. Perhaps one day we'll regularize psi abilities!

Here's something to think about. What if we decided as a species to value our phantastic supersensory intelligences (psi abilities) enough to bring them up from the undergrowth of our higher information processing capabilities so they wouldn't be hidden or repressed, but seen as 'normal?'

No Matter What Language

To use a recipe analogy to explain the 'taste' of full and complete Self-Realization, will be the same even if some of the words describing the secret to Self-Realization (recipe) appear in a slightly different font print. The enlightenment value, whether printed 'like this' or *like this* or **like this,** is the same.

Be a Little Zenful

It's okay if you want to be a little Zenful in your texting or in your emails, just avoid too many attachments.

Our Divine Coupling

We are the beneficiaries of a divine coupling at birth, when our Human Nature syncs with our Divine Nature.

Skin School Matriculation

While it is fitting to explore our temporal human experiences to gain the clarity and guidance we feel we need to master our skin school experiences, we also must be aware that examining our matriculation through challenging human experiences is important for our over-all soul growth and wellbeing.

Your Microcosomness

In the microcosm of your inner being, are the subtle vibrations of your molecular YOUniverse. You're composed of communes, colonies, cities and continents of trillions of cells in action. Your body is filled with cellular life. You are composed of hydrogen atoms and subatomic particles like quarks, leptons, and gluons that were present at the beginning of our universe.

You'll see that to simply describe your network of cells, your cellular family, as only biological containers comprised of a nucleus, membrane, receptors, tubes, fluid, and genetic markers is to miss the point of your biological footprint. You'll discover that your cells are highly intelligent beings with an innate divinity all their own.

Catching Up

Remember, in whatever dimension of being and in whatever form of beingness you find yourself, that dimension will be filled with magical things patiently waiting for your sentience and Supersentience to catch up!

Psinauts

Psinauts are similar to astronauts who are crew members of spaceflights in which they explore our universe—except *psinauts* are people who explore the deep, inner reaches of the psiverse.

Cul de Sacing

Have you ever felt like you've run around in circles, repeating the same old habits, making the same decisions, rerunning the same old tapes, reiterating the same outdated views of the world, rubber-stamping the same old excuses, rehashing the same old mistakes and missed opportunities. Leave that 'reel-ality' behind. Turn your back on the old REEL that keeps, you hamster-like, running in circles!

Darwin Was Onto Something

In his spectacular book, *The Blind Watchmaker*, Richard Dawkins predicts: "If a form of life is ever discovered in another part of the universe, however outlandish and weirdly alien that form of life may be in detail, it will be found to resemble life on Earth in one key aspect- it will have evolved by some kind of Darwinian natural selection."

I generally agree with Dawkins' view—with this proviso: If another form of extraterrestrial life discovers life on Earth, however 'outlandish and weirdly alien we may be in detail to that particular lifeform, it'll see that we'll resemble life in their part of the universe in one key respect—we'll have evolved, like them, by some kind of natural selection, that involves adaptive complexity, non-random reproduction, hereditary variation, and cumulative evolution by defined by slow gradualization.

What I've just outlined has been proven to occur. There are other conjectures, of course concerning the origin of life, one of which is the creationist's view of a primitive anthropomorphic deity who closely mimicked what happens during the legitimate—and proven—evolutionary process described above. Their deity's intervention can't be proven to be either true or untrue. In other words, it's what scientists call a nonfalsifiable argument.

However, all of the scientific evidence, to date, supports natural selection and not religious dogma. The odds against the instantaneous creation of perfect and whole human beings, or any other life form, including planets and universes, is, to use quantum physics reasoning 100 million, million, million, million to 1. To put it another way, remarkable claims require remarkable proof! To put it in yet another way—the origin of the concept of a primitive anthropomorphic, Creator God was itself the product of natural selection! It took billions of years to invent the God meme without offering one iota of proof that such a deity actually exists!

Meta-ing Beyond or About

Using 'meta' as a prefix puts you in a 'meta-universe' since 'meta' can mean "beyond," "after," "behind,' and even "about.' For example, metaphysics means "beyond the physical" or "about the physical"; metadata means "data about data"; from meta-joke we get "joke about jokes;" metapsychology means Psychology about psychology"; metamorphosis means "beyond a particular morphosus."

If you're happy and you know it, you know—without a shadow of a doubt—that you can find happiness in any *happen-ness.*

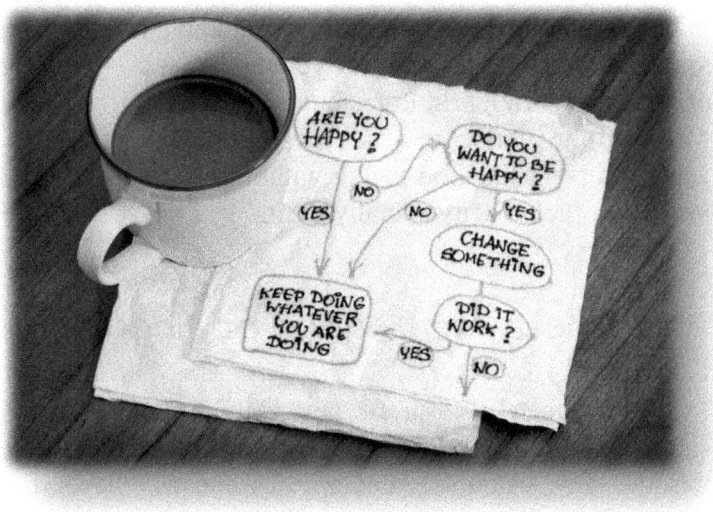

Cornered

Many people allow themselves to be cornered by a baying pack of dogmatic addicts who are predisposed to fiction instead of questioning the absurdities they champion.

Divinely Ordering Your Good

Divine Order isn't an external God-generated fiat or something a celestial deity imposes upon you. It isn't a predetermined God-decreed set of events, or prearranged deity-dictated succession of happenings, or preordained God-instituted installment of incidences.

It never has been! You may want to take a sobering breath, because there isn't any—and never has been—an external, primitive anthropomorphic God meme separate from you that has set our universe—or any of the multiverses—in motion.

Foreverness

You're born with the ability to transcend your physical dissolution. Your spiritual essence is timeless and immortal. There's a foreverness to your True Cosmic Nature. Allow that thought safe passage through your neuroverse. Grasp the higher Truth that there truly is a foreverness associated with your True Cosmic Nature that defines the scope and longevity of your eternal beingness.

Wandology

Your word is your wand, as they say. However, your positive, life-affirming, happy thoughts are your wandology!

Fearlessness

Fearlessness is casting off a part of us that doesn't work anymore—things like lack of confidence, bad habits, debilitating addictions, recurring doubts, chronic fears, and negative attitudes. Being fearless is listening to the 'acoustics of amnesty' which are the positive thoughts and feelings of relief, joy, and bliss you 'hear' when your mistakes are pardoned by your wise choices.

60 Seconds

Realize that for every minute you're pessimistic or cynical you lose 60 seconds of happiness.

Your Multidimensional Beingness

Your current life is one of the infinitesimal possibilities you embody on your way toward full and complete Self-Realization. You're a multidimensional being who travels through many veils of beingness. Some of which you allow to slow your nirvanic tendencies, and others which you fully embrace, allow you to accelerate your enlightenment.

Your multiplicity of physical embodiments are simply the garments you wear in each of your reincarnations and incarnations when you morph in-and-out of physicality. The multitudes of journeys into physical dimensions of beingness are the result of your desire to understand your true nature. They're part of your cosmic self-definitional quest.

The wonderful news is, whether you're experiencing the lives between physical lives part of your soul journey or, as is the case now, where you're in the particular physical embodiment you're enjoying today, every now moment is your Point of Power to gain the clarity you seek for your full and complete Self-Realization.

The Poise of Inner Peace

Be willing to release any attachment you have to anger, resentment, regret, or revenge for any hurtful thing someone has done to you—and what you may have done to yourself, so negative emotions don't form outposts in your consciousness. That's the true nature of forgiveness and the inner peace that comes with it!

One of the wonderful things about inner peace is that it's an antidote to despondency and depression, and a neutralizer of worry and irritation. See the confidence that comes from inner peace as a cognitive firewall that protects you from irrational thinking, ridiculous choices, and preposterous actions. So, bring the poise of your Divine Nature to the noise of outer circumstances. It's that poise that's silk for the soul!

Intention in Tension

Many people lose their intentions because they remain in tension. Indecisiveness filled with tension and inaction leads to what we call 'intention deficit disorder.'

The Blind Watchmaker

Creationists hypothesize that all living things (watches) were—and are—literally created and designed by the Master Watchmaker (God). However, those who don't subscribe to a primitive anthropomorphic 'designer deity' concept for the origins of life hold that the 'begetting' was—and continues to be—accomplished in gradual evolutionary stages by non-random natural selection.

Natural selection itself seems to be the 'blind watchmaker,' and natural selection is simply the idea that non-random reproduction (cumulative selection), hereditary variation, and step-by-step adaptation have consequences that continue to be far-reaching when there's time for them to be cumulative and unfold into more complex lifeforms.

Intuitive Wizdom*

Our Divine Nature, the Extraordinary Us, the Core Essence of Us, the One-of-a-kind-Us—is the Us that possesses the highest wizdom and inner knowing. Too often we are encouraged to seek answers to questions outside ourselves rather than explore our own inner wizdom. We're taught to find the expert, read a book, seek advice. But our journey is one of opening from the inside out, learning to look for answers, to go deep into our hearts and souls where we can connect with the inner wizdom and receive guidance from within to transform our lives.

*I spell the word 'wizdom' to represent inner wisdom as 'logic in a hurry.'

Our Concept of Time

I wonder if the concept of time is only Nature's way of preventing everything possible from happening all at once?

Your Do-ality

Celebrate your dual essences—your human beingness and your Cosmic Beingness... Your finite beingness and your Infinite Beingness... Your normal human abilities and your extrasensory human abilities... Your heart-centeredness and your thoughtfulness... Your sentience and your Supersentience. All of these dual essences are part of your eternal 'do-ality.'

Trans-Diaspora

I want to call your attention to an Eastern higher consciousness term. It's called MerKaBa. And translated into Egyptian parlance MerKaBa means: Mer (means light) Ka (means soul) and Ba (means body). However, it's referring to the concept of a Light Body that was known in that era. Your Light Body essence—and everybody's Light Body essence—was believed to be associated only with the 'transmigration of souls,' where our soul moves into another physical body after physical death. It's a novice understanding of reincarnation.

However, that definition of transmigration is much too limited when it comes to describing the full essence of our Light Body. So, Cher and I prefer the term 'trans-diaspora' which means interdimensional migration of intelligent beings. Just so you know, we're all experienced trans-diaspora souls, because we've incarnated and reincarnated many times into physical bodies and/or Ethereal Bodies in many dimensions of being.

Your localized human form—the one you're currently inhabiting– is the result of a series of lowered vibrations of your Higher Light Nature. Your physical body's lower vibration is your Human Nature. That means a vaster, more transcendental part of who you are is also part of your current life form. And that higher vibratory essence is your Super-Conscious Divine Nature.

Your Light Body's ethereal manifestation is known as your 'rainbow body' or 'chariot of the soul vehicle' and is your higher frequencied, individualized, Life Force that underwrites your physical beingness regardless of what dimension of being you choose to visit.

This timeless Light Body connects you to your encoded soul data through high electrical currents that assist you in translating and manifesting your hidden talents and soul purpose. As you activate, build and integrate your Light Body's characteristics, you reorganize your molecular structure and brain's neuroplasticity, permit your cellular mitochondria to absorb more light, and allow your body to be less dense and more free to express itself inter-dimensionally. (For more detailed information see our *Light Body White Light Paper* located in our Holton Product Mall).

A Love-Filled Life

I firmly believe a genuinely fulfilling and love-filled life is available to all of us—if we raise our consciousness above the din of disbelief… above the feeling that we can't experience the depth of love that we've had before or can still have.

Any and All Forms of Dogmafication

Religious fundamentalists, and any other dogmatic profession, are deeply enamored with their form of dogmatic asphyxiation, because they've been taught (by each other) to perpetuate their strongly entrenched confirmation bias.

Juneteenth

My birthday date (June 19th) was named Juneteenth, a National Federal Holiday commemorating the anniversary of the end of slavery in the United States on June 19,1865. It has special meaning for me, in addition to its fantastic original intent. As I look back on my life, I realize I've always advocated an end to all forms of slavery—being a slave to: religious, and all other forms of dogma; confirmation biases; negativity; inequality; lying and stealing; prejudice; believing in fiction instead of the truth; etc.

Our Homo Genusness

One of my ph!losoph!cal !ncl!nat!ons took me to this hypothetical musing after I read about transhumanism and posthumanism in a Bioethics and Transhumanism article in *The Journal of Medicine and Philosophy* and several articles in the *Journal of Posthuman Studies* on my birthday in 2021: What if, once we evolve into the Homo transhumanis[1] species and Homo posthumanis[2] species (I've coined those two species names), they'll be considered as part of the genus Homo[3] as are Homo sapiens, Homo erectus, Homo habilis, Homo rhodesienis, Homo neanderthalenois, Homo naledi, Homo georgicus, Homo ergaster, Homo longi (Dragon Man), etc.? Cher and I pose this philosophical musing because we believe our transhuman and posthuman statuses are both in our future. Check it out for yourself and see if you agree!

[1] Transhuman is a human sapiens who has 'evolved' beyond our current physical and mental limitations by means of science and technology.

[2] Posthuman is a transhuman who has 'totally evolved' beyond transhuman silicone-based physical embodiment which has been replaced completely by artificial technologies.

[3] Homo genus is defined as the family Hominidae (order Primates) which is characterized by a relatively large cranial capacity, limb structure that's adapted to a habitual erect posture, a bipedal gait, well-developed and fully opposable thumbs, hands that are capable of power and precision grips, and the ability to make precision tools and implements.

Forging Links

To forge links … going beyond the given … to see hidden patterns and inter-relationships, and uncovering different contexts are all open sesames to different perspectives … divergent lines of thought … playful nuancing … and just plain old fun. Just know, that part of the fun in expanding contexts is the way to find hidden knowledge … to encounter amazing horizons. It's creatively and playfully juxtapositioning … linking … allegorizing … contrasting … comparing … partnering … even the cahooting of what is … to discover what can be.

Meditation's Perks

Recognize that meditation—whether it's a Sitting Meditation … or a Walking Meditation … or a 12 Power Meditation … or a 13th Power Meditation …or a focused Eating Meditation … or an Insight Meditation … or a

Guided Meditation—is an inner focus practice that connects the temporal, flesh-and-blood skin school you with the ethereal, transcendental, spiritual you. It moves you from the finite you to the infinite you; from the small 'c' conscious you to the capital 'C' Conscious you; from the unenlightened you to the enlightened you; from the dogmatic you to the questioning unquestioned answers you; from the subconscious you to the Super-Conscious you.

The Power of the !ncl!ne

The important thing you need to know about thoughts is that your thoughts determine your !ncl!nat!ons, your !ncl!nat!ons lead to your preferences, your preferences lead to your choices, and your choices lead to your actions.

The Law of Mind Action

Are you familiar with the Law of Mind Action expression: 'Thoughts held in mind produce after their kind?' It's a commonly-used expression by many New Thought people. The question is, however: Thoughts produce what after their kind?

The answer seems obvious, but I'm going to say it anyway: They produce similar thoughts and feelings. That is, they lead to thoughts which are characteristic of the consciousness which spawned them in the first place. That means that similar thoughts and associated feelings, repeated often enough, can reinforce truth or perpetuate error.

That's how thoughts travel through your mind and that's how thoughts are 'auctioned off' too! When you control your thinking you control your thoughts. If you auction your thinking to the world of outer appearances, you essentially auction your life off to the world of wishcraft, movement toward quick fixes, and 'too good to be true' schemes.

Limitation-Free

You can turn any limiting beliefs you may have into limitless achievements by remembering that your own field of vision may not represent the limits of your own incredible potential. While your human body may have certain limits, your consciousness is limitless ... expansive ... unconfined ... infinite ... timeless ... immortal ... and constantly filled with endless possibilities. You're more limitation-free than you know. Moving forward, beyond any stale beliefs and patterns is heroic ... and soul enriching ... and life defining.

New Beginnings

At one time or another, we've all had to move from a disappointing past into a hopeful future—from what was ... to what's next ... taking the current us with us. The heaviness of the past is replaced by the lightness of beginning anew, of forging a future that's kinder and gentler, of orchestrating a more positive and resilient you, a you that's determined to find the happiness you know is waiting around the corner for you.

The first step towards a new beginning is to decide you're not going to stay where you are. That decision in and of itself is celebrating endings, because they precede new beginnings. Remind yourself not to wait until the conditions are perfect to begin anew, because it's the new beginning that'll make the conditions perfect.

Recognize that your current circumstances don't limit where you can go. They merely determine where your next steps lead you. And the good thing—one of the many good things about new beginnings is, that they can become gateways to a happier, more fulfilling life. Soo, never underestimate the power you have to take your life in a more fulfilling direction.

Cognitive Skyhooks

I'm going to use an aeronautical term called 'skyhook' as a metaphor to describe a higher consciousness state of being. Here's what skyhooks are and then I'll analogize their usefulness to our Superconsciousness: Skyhooks* are imaginary aeronautical geostationary contrivances (orbiting satellites which can fling rocket ships out of Earth's atmosphere into outer space) which could be also be used to suspend technologies (cameras, telescopes, antennas, etc.), permanently in the sky for surveillance.

Here's my !ncl!nat!on to use skyhooks as an analogy for living in the higher order atmospherics of Supersentient thinking. Highly imaginative and creative people (who are perpetually metaphorically and figuratively-inclined) seem to have highly conscious 'cognitive skyhooks' that keep the higher order thinking processes in their neuroverse lifted above most people's Earthbound cognitive range—that is, people who seldom or never use 'cognitive skyhooks.'

* Skyhooks got their name from a fictional organization in the 1956 film *Earth vs. the Flying Saucers.*

A Place of Reference

Pursue what catches your heart. Remember … the past is a place of reference, not a place of residence.

Paths Re-Chosen

Because we're spiritual beings having a human experience, we have access to a number of paths: the infinite, more transcendental paths chosen and not chosen… often chosen and less chosen … re-chosen and never chosen. Whatever path you take, make it one that contributes to your Greater Good and the Greater Good of humankind.

Fact Checking

When presented with verifiable facts, we can change our mind—and our meme.

Heir Power

Remind yourself often that you're one with the One Presence (Omnipresent Universal Reality, Pure Universal Consciousness, the All, the Infinite Isness) and can live joyfully and healthily, and prosperously at the speed of your Divine Nature… because you have incredible heir power—that's HEIR POWER—due to the eternality of your Divine Genealogy which is, and always has been, ever-present in your DNA.

Gifting Yourself

Holding onto the past keeps you from moving comfortably into the future, just like an inbreath prevents you from welcoming the next inbreath, unless you expel the old inbreath. Your old way of thinking is only a shadow of the new you. And the old shadow is fading and can become a nonexistent remnant of the current you ... the new you. Making room for the new, helps you get past the past, and see the present as a present, as gifting yourself with the new, more evolved you.

The Sacred Path

Understand that your present sojourn in skin school is as much about unlearning what you've been taught by the greater society in which you're a part of, which has opted many centuries ago to prefer a religious mindset over a transformative spiritual perspective.

Questioning those conventional answers and arriving at spiritual truths will increase the depth and bandwidth of your thinking, being and doing... so you can see your greater good and the greater good of humankind.

As you awaken to your spirituality and walk the sacred path toward a higher consciousness state of beingness, your progress is up to you. You don't have to be limited by anything external to you. The clarity you need to matriculate through this skin school experience is within.

And it comes from mastering your thoughts, intentions, feelings, choices and actions; by trusting in your own knowledge, and understanding, and experience of the nature of Omnipresent Universal Reality; and trusting in the knowledge and experience of other like-minded people who care about you, and want you to succeed. It means being happy, to experience inner peace, to find the joy that leads to healthy, positive and prosperous living.

A Renaissance in Thinking

Unabashedly affirm a constant renaissance in your thinking, being, and doing... and wear your persistent thriveability on your entire demeanor. Let people see it in your eyes ... in your contagious smile ... in the way you carry yourself ... in the energy you exhibit ... in the passion for life you outpicture by your actions.

You've Booked Your Physicality

As an eternal spiritual being you've booked this temporary skin school experience. Sooo, make it one of your bestsellers, no matter what happens to you down here (a lower vibrational dimension of beingness), on your way to total and complete enlightenment (a higher vibrational dimension of beingness).

Well-thiness

I invite you to make life-affirming wellness traits like the following *well*-thiness cocktail to define your health and well-beingness: Traits like positivity and optimism ... joyfulness ... cheerfulness ... loving kindness ... compassion ... intuitive wisdom ... open-mindedness ... curiosity ... good-naturedness ... forgiveness ... sense of wonder ... heart-centeredness ... inner strength ... playfulness ... courage ... morality and ethics ... generosity ... and happiness—so you can kick negativity to the curb every chance you get.

Archipelago Experiences

Each of our skin school incarnations and reincarnations is an archipelago* experience in our matriculation toward Self-Realization.

> * Archipelago - a group or scattering of similar things in a large space (an expanse of water with many scattered islands; a group of small islands in a huge lake; Florida Keys, Bahamas, Japan; and by analogy - small parks within a city, stores and kiosks within a mall, etc.).

Truth Tripping

When I first thought of this post I considered calling it a 'Truth Triage.' However, I think you'll see that 'Truth Tripping' seems a little more appropriate. It seems to me that definitions by Merriam-Webster, Dictionary.com, Oxford and Cambridge Dictionaries, and Macmillan, etc., don't go quite far enough.

Here are snapshots of a few ph!losoph!cal !ncl!nat!ons on 'truth': Truth is what is and what isn't! It's what exists and can exist, and what doesn't exist and either can't or won't exist. It's what has happened and what hasn't happened. Truth is both evidence-based and evidence-defaced. Truth is always scientifically falsifiable (can be proven either a truth or a falsehood). The truth is what happens and doesn't happen. The truth is what's inescapable. Truth is the Omnipresent Universal Reality, the Greater Reality, the Only True Reality.

Liberation From Maya

There's no path to enlightenment and liberation from maya (illusion) that doesn't pass through questioning unquestioned answers mileposts.

Your Emancipatory Grail

The power of choice will always be your emancipatory grail. It'll liberate you from what you need to be liberated from, and take you to where you need to be directed toward. How close you come to your Authentic Self is up to you. The only limits you have are those you place on yourself. The real choice is: will you use more willpower than won't power when it comes to achieving the inner harmony and illumination that leads to Self-Realization?

A Dose of Reality

Reality is the main cause of stress to those who have PhDs in fabrication, lies, disinformation, and fiction.

Religious Troglobiting

Evolutionary biologists call animals that live only in the darkest parts of caves, and essentially become blind— troglobites.* These animals and insects have chosen to live in perpetual darkness. Religious fundamentalists and creationists have become 'religious troglobites' because of their debilitating dogmatic perspective.

By analogy, people who live in the perpetual darkness of entrenched confirmation biases, idiotic paradigms, and uncompromising dogmas, have become blind to truth. For example, in the case of religious fundamentalists and creationists, who believe in a primitive anthropomorphic God meme that isn't real—and never has been real—they seem to have a blind spot. Their concept of God (usually referred to as a He) is a fictional character perpetuated to control the faithful by selling fear, guilt and shame. Their 'religious troglobiting' is keeping millions of people in the dark!

* You may find it interesting to know that a related term (troglodyte) which I've mentioned previously, refers to a human being cave dweller or one who inhabits the area beneath the overhanging rocks of a cliff.

What a Wonderful World

Unfortunately, the considerable vices of a segment of humankind continue to be quite active and perennially perpetual as agents of conscienceless depopulation, destructiveness, and perhaps precursors of our eventual extinction.* However, our saving grace may very well be an evolved capacity to champion truth over lies, and evidence-based facts over evidence-barren misrepresentations. What a wonderful world that would be!

*Cosmologists sooth that humankind will become extinct in another 7.8 billion years, or perhaps a little sooner.

Eggs-actly

I'm going to mention the Second Law of Thermodynamics as it relates to this particular post. The Second Law of Thermodynamics states that as energy is

233

transferred or transformed, more and more of it is wasted, and that there's a natural tendency of any isolated system to degenerate into a more disordered state which is irreversible. It's linked with the First Law of Thermodynamics which will serve as the background for this particular post. The First Law of Thermodynamics states that because energy can't be created or destroyed, the total *quantity* of energy in the universe stays the same.

Okay. Here we go! According to the Second Law of Thermodynamics, you can't unscramble a scrambled egg! Sounds like a no-brainer, doesn't it? And so does the well-known toothpaste example.* However, in all due respect to the 'Second Law' neither is irreversible! And here's 'eggs-actly' why: If you feed a hen a scrambled egg, the hen will be able to make a perfectly formed 'unscrambled' egg when it lays its next egg. In fact, chickens can eat all parts of an egg (raw or cooked), and eggs are very good sources of protein and calcium for chickens! Sooo, eggs can easily be unscrambled!

As far as the toothpaste example goes, it was Harry Robbins Haldeman, Chief of Staff to President Richard Nixon, who absent-mindedly said: "You can't put the toothpaste back in the tube." The truth is—you can put toothpaste back into the tube—in a number of ways!

I'll mention a few, and if you're interested, simply Google 'How do you put toothpaste back in a tube' and you'll be surprised at people's ingenuity. Here' one:

A pediatric dentist offered this solution: Put the cap on and cut the lower part of the crimped end off with sharp scissors. Use a spatula to put the toothpaste back into the lower end of the tube. Clean and dry (inside and out) the cut end. Use a hot iron to reseal the lower end of the tube. And voilà, the paste is tubed!

A dental hygienist shares how she 'squeezed' the Second Law of Thermodynamics: If it's a small amount of paste and it's not a new tube of toothpaste, slowly squeeze the flattened sides of the tube while sticking the open end deep into the amount you want to return to the tube. The squeezing action creates a vacuum as the tube becomes more round and this allows the paste to be sucked back into the tube. It may not suck in all of the paste you want but it does return a goodly amount of paste back into the tube.

There are more innovative solutions, as I indicated above, so don't hesitate to challenge other unquestioned answers which is one of the themes of this book.

*You've probably also heard that you can't put toothpaste back into its tube.

Carte Blanche Anthropomorphization

There's a strong !ncl!nat!on in human nature to anthropomorphize external objects with the same qualities and characteristics it observes in itself—including its manufactured anthropomorphic God meme.

Intercellular Genetic Space

When you think about it, we're surrounded by interstellar space, hyperspace,* and genetic space! The actual life forms that currently exist here, as of this writing, and that have ever lived on Earth—and in interstellar space and hyperspace—are a tiny subset of the theoretical life forms that could have existed, and then evolved had they existed.

* Hyperspace is a concept from cutting-edge science and science fiction that co-exists with our own universe, and yet relates to higher dimensions and superluminal methods of interstellar travel.

A Time Warp

Has it occurred to you that today is the tomorrow you thought about yesterday?

I Blink, You Blink, We All Blink

All of us human beings, including those with 20-20 vision, are partially blind. Our eye blink takes about 50 milliseconds. Sooo, that means we're blind about 5% of the time when we're awake and have our eyes open normally. And, you might ask, why have we evolved so that we blink with both eyes simultaneously? Why haven't we evolved to have alternate eye blinks which would mean we'd be able to have 100% instead of 95% visibility all of the time we have our eyes open? Alternate eye blinks would also save us energy.

Human Evolution

The current version of humankind is the product of evolutionary speciation. We haven't evolved to remain in our present biologic, carbon-based state any more than a caterpillar has evolved to remain a caterpillar.

Erring Less and Less

When you err less, then err less again, and then continue to err less, you'll eventually reach Self-Realization, because you've erred-out an unenlightened ego!

Sleeping Sickness

Sleeping sickness is a neuropsychiatric disease that causes sleep disruption, lethargy, confusion, and even convulsions. Its rural African form is transmitted by tsetse flies, and can be fatal if left untreated. It's occurred to me that there's a prevalent type of non-tsetse fly related sleeping sickness that infects highly complacent and dogmatic people who are 'bitten' by certain airborne beliefs that aren't questioned as to their veracity or truthfulness when they're circulated widely in certain gullible circles. Believing in these types of toxic dogmas puts many susceptible people to sleep and can be fatal to their open-mindedness, ability to separate truth from fiction, and higher order thinking.

How Robotic Are We?

What if we're made of gazillions of micromolecular genetic machines (robots)? Well, you can take the 'what if' out of that sentence! Many people worldwide are already equipped with cancer-fighting, neurological and cardiovascular therapy, and vaccine delivery nanobots and shape-shifting microrobots that swim through blood vessels delivering life-saving drugs.

These programmable itty bitty bots (microbristle bots or vibrots) measure just 1 to 2 millimeters (0.39 - 0.08 inch) and are a fraction if the size of a grain of sand. They're powered by acoustic and ultrasound waves and/o solar cells, and swim through our bioverse looking for signs of illness or injury, taking tissue samples, and repairing the body. Fascinating, huh!

Roboscientists (that's what I call them) are already exploring how to build sophisticated microcircuitry that make these minibots programmable so they can run without human intervention. Because these itty bot's 'brains' are based on classical electronic circuits, their next generational bots will be smarter! I'm gobsmacked at the future implications of these nanotechnologies!

Physicist Richard Feynman thought of what he called 'swallowable surgeons' in 1959 that could roam the human body and perform surgeries on demand! Where will these microbots take us? Right now, it depends on where we want to take them! Perhaps in ten years, it'll depend on where they want to take us! As I think about it, the future nanobot possibilities have created a thought salad in my head, and my excitement goes from 'ma head to-ma-toes!'

Our Eternal Etherealness

We have all evolved into the womb of matter from our Ethereal Universal Eternality, which makes us 'in the physical world, but not of the physical world.'

Ph!losoph!cod!pp!ty

Ph!losoph!cod!pp!ty is a word I've coined to describe dipping into a philosophical mindset that arrives at timeless transcendental insights.

A Pain in the Ask

Sitting too long without questioning why you're sitting so long must be a pain in the ask.

Outliers and Out-and-Out Liars

All religions, professions, disciplines, institutions, organizations, traditions, establishments, societies, etc., have both outliers and out-and-out liars!

Truth Stonewalled

Truth is ignored when it finds itself up against highly dogmatic-smeared beliefs, ruthless hidden agendas, mindless confirmation biases, and corrupt ulterior motives.

Our Global and Interstellar Citizenship

We're global citizens of not only our world, but interstellar citizens of our universe, and the multiverse, and many other dimensions in the cosmos. Unfortunately, many people—most people—don't know it. One day, I believe we'll be universe and multiverse hopping, because we'll have SuperSentient Consciousness abilities!

Endings and Beginnings

Where a black hole in space ends, a white hole begins. Perhaps the same analogy can fit where a telescope ends, a microscope begins.

Speciation

This may sound suspicious, but religion has many species: Methodists, Baptists, Catholics, Judaism, Seventh Day Adventists, Pentecostals, Lutherans, Quakers, Buddhists, Hindus, Taoists, Jainists, Sufists, Islam, Zoroastrianism, New Thought, Bahá'í, etc.

Science has many species, too: psychology, neuroscience, sociology, epigenetics, aeronautics, cosmology, spectrology, aerobiology, evolutionary biology, robotics, genetics, biophysics, irenology, ecophysiology, epidemiology, catacoustics, paradoxology, quantum physics, dactylography, helioseismology, anesthesiology, cytomorphology, exobiology (also - astrobiology), evolutionary neuropsychology, zoosemiotics, virology, anthropology, uranology, astrobiology, paleoanthropology, kinesiology, parapsychology, zooarchaeology, etc.—to name only a few.

Ph!losoph!cal Footnotes

The obvious generalization to make concerning our current modern day ph!losoph!cal !ncl!nat!ons, that include my own, is that they're a series of footnotes of our ancestors' footnotes, which were a series of footnotes of their ancestors' footnotes, which were a series …

Post Traumatic Religious Experience Disorder (PTRE)

PTRED is a religious experience disorder in which a person has difficulty recovering after experiencing or witnessing a terrifying religious indoctrination. The condition may last months or years, with triggers that can bring back memories of the trauma accompanied by intense emotional and physical reactions.

Symptoms may include nightmares or unwanted memories of the trauma, avoidance of situations that bring back memories of traumatic events, heightened anxiety and depression. Treatment includes different types of post trauma-focused psychotherapies like seeking a more spiritually-oriented higher consciousness path, meditation, forgiveness counseling, etc.

It's in the Details

Omnipresent Universal Reality is more, much more, than just in the details. It underwrites all of them.

Forbidden Fruit

Whether it's a bite or a byte, the proverbial 'forbidden fruit' is simply a metaphor for what I believe the real 'forbidden fruit' is: the outlandish dogmas of all kinds which proselytize untruths and out-and-out lies of all kinds. These obnoxious untruths may 'taste good' for a while until you find out that they're sour, evidence-barren fictions instead of delicious, evidence-based facts. Forbidden 'fruits' (dogmas, false beliefs, superstitions, irrational shibboleths, etc.) retail errors and falsehoods instead of truths.

Our Neuroverse

If our entire body is a neuroverse, we think, reason, and process information with our entire body, not just with our brain.

Circumambulating

The interesting thing about ph!losoph!cal !ncl!nat!ons is that many of them, ministerially speaking, give you an opportunity to circumambulate (build your life mindfully around) Divine Ideas and hidden realities long enough to get a sense for their deeper universal meanings.

Herd Community

Writing this particular post during the 2020-2022 Covid pandemic prompted me to strike a comparison between the immunological 'herd immunity'[1] and psychosocial 'herd community[2]' as they respectfully refer to the pandemic and science research. In both cases, when you follow the 'herd,' you have to watch where you step! What does your 'herd instinct' say about that?

[1] Herd immunity is a form of indirect protection from infectious disease that can occur with some diseases when a sufficient percentage of an affected population becomes immune to an infection, whether it's through previous infections or vaccinations, thereby reducing the likelihood of infection for those who lack immunity.

[2] Herd community or 'herd effect' describes the way scientists 'herd' together and arrive at mutual agreements about which research methodologies will or will not be deemed acceptable.

Passport Portals

I see my ph!losoph!cal !ncl!nat!ons (like my astonishing mystical experiences, OBEs, lucid dreams, hypnopompic visualizations, and revelations), as a passport into higher realms of thought and expanded consciousness.

Policing My Philosophizing

My philosophizing is policed by my penchant for wrapping it around evidence-based science, uncommon sense, accumulated knowledge, intuition, discernment, and questioning unquestioned answers. Otherwise, it would only be an echo of other people's voices.

Ph!losophy's Mojo

One of the neat things about ph!losophy is that its movement is usually toward the light instead of the darkness, generally toward unraveling things instead of tying things up, ordinarily toward questioning unquestioning answers instead of perpetuating unquestioned answers.

Fictional Art

From my way of thinking, certain pieces of what's mindlessly referred to as art are whatever you can get away with.

Speciation's Dilemma

What if our world—you know, planet Earth—hasn't specifically evolved for the success and domination by one particular species?

Parabolic Incl!nat!ons

The more I get involved in ph!losoph!cal pursuits, I realize that my learning curve is more like a parabola. Like a parabola, ph!losophy has no end points and its bandwidth extends infinitely to the left, and the right, and upward toward Ultimate Truths.

Unrepeatability Replicated

One of the chief criticisms of psi research is its seeming unrepeatability! What if its laboratory psi unrepeatability is an inherent unrepeatability of psi-ness? Traditional science wants psi abilities demonstrated on-demand in laboratory settings, which complicates the investigative process. If that's the case, our attempts to understand the nature of much of our universe's unrepeatability should be met with the same criticism. Don't you think?

Neutralizing Open-Mindedness

It appears that (I could be wrong, but I believe I'm right) the number one aim of fundamental religious bafflegab has been, and continues to be, the complete and absolute neutralization of the open-minded questioning of any and all of the unquestioned answers retailed by that particular belief system.

Credible Evidence

As a MetaSpiritual Unity minister, ph!losopher, and science fan who trusts in evidence-based science and believes in evolutionary natural selection to explain our being here, I know exactly what it would take to change my mind—credible evidence that refutes my belief.

Consolation Prize

It should come as no surprise that the consolation (comfort, solace, palliative) value of highly dogmatic beliefs, supported by the confirmation biases that reinforce their misinformation and disinformation, do not—and never have—raised their truth value one iota above the absurd. Confirmation biases and highly dogmatic truancy are both archaic sclerotic* belief systems.

> *Sclerotic means being highly rigid and losing the ability to adapt.

Imagine, Just Imagine

Remember John Lennon's incredible song *Imagine*? I think it's incredible! One of its key lyrics postures 'a world with no religion, too.' It certainly gave me pause when I first heard it sung—as I'm sure it has for millions of people. However, I invite you to think about the implications of what the disastrous fruits of fundamentalist religions have been throughout the centuries.

It should come as no surprise that, in the name of religion, there've been many untoward immoral acts performed against people, organizations, cultures, societies, and concurrent religions. What would the world be today without a history of religion-based conflicts—or propagated by soooo many species of religions?

Imagine: no 'just war' doctrine of Augustine and Aquinas, no Cathar inquisition, no crusades, no drowning or burning women at the stake during witch hunts, no persecution of Jews as 'Christ killers,' no Albigensian genocide, no Israeli/Palestinian wars, no Serb/Croat/Muslim massacres, no 'holy wars' in the Middle East, no rampant global jihads, no al-Qaida attacks on 9-11, no burning

Planned Parenthood Centers, no church's immorality against women and the LGBTQ2+ community, no church's condemnation of spiritual/not religious communities, etc.

The Apple of My I

Here's some 'food' for thought. It wasn't an 'apple' which the Biblical Adam and Eve couple were supposed to have eaten. Actually, if the truth be told, it wasn't an apple. Just so you know, the Hebrew Bible doesn't specify what type of fruit the couple was supposed to have eaten, and there's no indication that it was an apple. The Hebrew word used in that verse is 'peri,' a generic word for fruit, in general. And, the modern day Hebrew word for apple is 'tapuach,' which doesn't appear anywhere in Genesis. By the way, 'tapuach' also means generic fruit.

The 'fruit' most likely could have been grapes, a fig, or citron (lemon-like fruit), but certainly not the proverbial apple—because apples aren't even from the Middle East (They're from Kazakhstan in Central Asia). In *Paradise Lost*, Milton describes the fruit Eve tasted as being "fuzzy on the outside and juicy, sweet and ambrosial." Now, that's just 'peachy,' don't you think?

Tower of Babel

Suppose AI technology is our 21st century Tower of Babel? We've broken plenty of silicone-based ground alright; however, our carbon-based intellect isn't catching up fast enough with the speed of our technological growth. The bandwidth of our current ethics and morality doesn't seem sufficient to understand the languaging of the smart technologies we're creating.

Grand Designer Memeology

Where did the proverbial Grand Designer God (the current religious, primitive anthropomorphic Judeo-Christian God meme) come from? Was 'He' (This God is generally referred to as a 'He') designed by a 'Grand Designer' that was also primitively anthropomorphic? Was that Grand Designer God meme also designed by a primitive predecessor anthropomorphic male 'Grand Designer?' Where did those predecessor Gods come from—if there were, in fact, predecessor God memes?

It appears that finite physicality has both beginnings and an endings. Does infinite etherealness have beginnings and ends, too? To what extent are the 'Designer Gods' mentioned above alpha and omegatized? Does being free from the limitations of spacetime necessarily mean being immune from beginningness and endlessness? It makes sense that universes probably have beginnings (big bangs) and endings (collapsing into singularities); however, what about multiverses and megaverses? Are they, like the 'Designer Gods' above, thought to be exempt from having beginnings and endings? Or do those alpha and omegatized quantum states only apply to their physicality?

I can confirm that this Grand Designer Memeology post has a beginning and an end as far as the text itself goes! However, I suspect that the ad infinitum nature of the questions I've asked may linger indefinitely.

Snooze Button

The unfortunate thing about dogmas is that they ask you to hit the 'snooze button.'

Solipsistically Speaking

During one of my ph!losoph!cal bents, which was especially mindboggling, I asked my Higher Self if it was just a solipsistic* experience gone haywire, or just me?

> * Solipsistic is a philosophical idea that only one's mind is sure to exist.

Persistent Dogmafication

Persistent dogmafication unabashedly nurtures 'cartels' of evidence-barren fictional beliefs that are plonked around carelessly hoping people won't fact check them.

Digital Immortality

When you think about it, we are immortal beings in many different kinds of speciation: pre-human sentient speciation, human carbon-based speciation, transhuman silicon-based speciation, posthuman digitized speciation without biological chains, transgenic* human speciation, etc.

> *Gene transfer from one human being to another via genetic engineering.

Smartness

We've got smart phones, smart TVs, smart nanobots, smart kitchen appliances, smart watches, smart keys, smart 'dust,' smart houses, etc. There're come a time—not in the too distant future—that we'll have smart physical bodies that house a smart neuroverse and bioverse that'll be connected with 'IoT' (the Internet of Things).

Will that smartness come from smart technologies, interconnectivity with the Internet? Artificial intelligence? Be app-driven? Wi-Fi activated? Or a combination of all of the above? YES! After all the term 's.m.a.r.t' that describes smart technology is an acronym: Self-Monitoring Analysis and Reporting Technology!

Opposites

For every evidence-based, truth-seeking spiritual teacher, there seems to be an opposite evidence-barren, dogmatic religious minister.

Global Brain

The Cloud-Based Global Brain, a sort of syntellect,* is coming! That may sound like ph!losoph!cal !ntox!cation, however, it's a sobering thought! Why? Because it's already being conceptualized and technologically pursued. The Global Brain is seen as a neuroscience-inspired single information processing internet system that connects all humans and functions as part of the collective 'nervous system' of the planet.

The 'Global brain' was coined in 1982 by Peter Russell in his book Global Brain. In 1945, Pierre Teilhard de Chardin described the emergence of a 'noosphere,' or 'global brain' as an inevitable microbiological planetization! Evolutionary biologist, historian, and author, H.G. Wells, described a synthetic World Brain as a permanent 'World Encyclopaedia' that will provide universal information resources worldwide. Proponents say look for the Global Brain to be up and running by 2100!

Here's a ph!losoph!cal thought. What if our thoughts, feelings, memories, and personality characteristics could be 'downloaded' into a computer, robot, or even a Homo synth, or Homo siliconensis. (See my post *Homo Sapiens or Homo synth* which follows this post). This would allow our 'essential self' to survive after our physical, carbon-based body dies as a silicone-based cybernetic simulacrum (an imitation of something).

> *Syntellect is the unified mind of civilization that integrates all individual natural and artificial minds through the accumulative effects of informational networks.

From a Neutrino's Perspective

When we evolve into Supersentience, our brains will be equipped to visualize what it would be like to pass through barriers like a wall, or whatever 'solid' object we choose, including the Earth itself, just like neutrinos pass through them. Imagine how it would *feeeel* neutrinoizing through billions of miles of interstellar space faster than the speed of light before breakfast and still be home for dinner!

Removing All Doubt

It's a well-known fact that light travels faster than sound. That's why some people may appear bright before they open their mouth and say something!

Psychic-Active

It's occurred to me that people who have had—and continue to have—psychic experiences are 'psychic-active.'

A Dash of Sass to Wrap Things Up

Dance. Smile. Laugh. Giggle. Joke. Trust. Ph!losoph!ze. Risk. Hope. Love. Wish. Believe. Question unquestioned answers. Challenge. Explore. Think outside the box. Speculate. Venture. Dare to. Speak your truth, etc.

Most of all, enjoy every consecutive-moment-of-now of your skin school journey, and appreciate where you are in each moment instead of focusing on how far you have to go.

###

Blessings to you and kudos for your ph!losoph!cal interests in discovering deeper truths.

Here's one perennial truth I wholeheartedly recommend that appears on my book cover. I hope this maxim will stick in your mind long after you finish this book:

Always bring the poise of your Divine Nature to the noise of materiality.

About Rev. Dr. Bil Holton

Rev. Dr. Bil Holton has been writing, speaking, coaching, and publishing for over 35 years. As a MetaSpiritual Thought Leader, ordained Unity minister, 21st Century metaphysician, and student of science and spirituality, Rev. Bil has a solid reputation for his strength of character, engaging personality, out-of-the-box thinking, and strong work ethic. His extraordinary metaphysical teachings and his ability to bring spiritual Truths into clarity by combining science, psience, and spirituality put him in high demand as a teacher and spiritual coach.

When he isn't involved in neuroscience research, studies in quantum physics, and metaphysical writing, Bil enjoys golf, travel, ballroom dancing, jigsaw puzzles, the theatre, and landscaping. Rev. Bil, together with his wife and business partner, Rev. Cher Holton, cofounded The Global Center for Spiritual Awakening and Unity Center for

YOUniversal Prosperity, with a mission to help people master the art of "living in skin school" by walking the spiritual path on practical, positive, prosperous feet.

On a personal note:

Bil and Cher take what they call "Indiana Jones Experiences" including white-water rafting, sky-diving, helicopter fly-bys and even fire walking to push their risk-taking envelopes. But one of their most exciting adventures led them into the world of ballroom dancing, where they have competed on a national level and participated in many showcases! They are amateur student couple champions in several ballroom dance categories—and even have a ballroom dance floor in their home!

The Holtons live in North Carolina, and enjoy friends and family who all bring much love and laughter to their lives!

Other Spiritually-Oriented Books by Rev. Dr. Bil Holton:

The Gospel of Matthew, New Metaphysical Version
The Gospel of Mark, New Metaphysical Version
The Gospel of Luke, New Metaphysical Version
The Gospel of John, New Metaphysical Version
The Book of Revelation, New Metaphysical Version
Rev. Bil Unplugged and Unedited
Ruff-Housing with Religious Dogma
My Mystical Moments Musings: A 21st Century Mystic's Perspective
*How to Achieve YOUniversal Prosperity and Experience Health,
    Happiness, Inner Peace, and Financial Freedom ... in less time
    than you might think!**
*Spiritually Speaking: A Metaphysical Interpretation of Spiritual,
    Religious, and Modern Day Secular Terms (for those who are
    more spiritual than religious)**
*Reconciling the Church's Science Phobia: The Dance Between
    Science and Spirituality**
Straight Talk About Spiritual Stuff*
Crackerjack Choices: 200 of the Best Choices You Will Ever Make*
*Right Thoughts, Right Choices, Right Actions: 200 of the Best
    Choices Unity People Will Ever Make**
Life Changing Spiritual Practices, Volumes 1-12*
Business Prayers for Millennium Managers*
Get Over It! The Truth About What You Know That Just Ain't So**
*Get Over These, Too! More Truth About What You Know That Just
    Ain't So!***
*Power Up Your Life! Accessing Your Twelve Powers to Achieve
    Health, Happiness, Abundance, & Inner Peace****

*   *Co-authored with Rev. Dr. Cher Holton*
**   *Co-authored with Rev. Dr. Paul Hasselbeck*
*** *Co-authored with Rev. Dr. Cher Holton and Rev. Dr. Paul
       Hasselbeck*

Connect With Bil Holton

Follow me on X (formerly known as Twitter):
https://x.com/metaphysicalweb

Friend me on Facebook:
https://facebook.com/GCSAcommunity

Favorite me at Smashwords:
https://smashwords.com/profile/view/bilholton

Subscribe to our blog:
https://GCSAcommunity.org/blog-resources

Visit our Higher Consciousness GCSA Academy:
https://GCSAacademy.com

Ordering/Speaking Information:

To order copies of Rev. Dr. Holton's books, and request information about scheduling him for speaking engagements: Visit HoltonProductMall.com or call 919.530.9417

Photo Credits

[Used with permission]

Ph!losoph!cal Explorations
Table of Contents

Note: Because of the lengthiness of this Table of Contents, which lists each entry by name, it is included in the back of the book for your convenience in finding items of interest.

259

271

www.ingramcontent.com/pod-product-compliance
Lightning Source LLC
Chambersburg PA
CBHW052032090426
42739CB00010B/1878